In May 1980, the <u>QE2</u> greets the refurbished <u>Norway</u> in New York Harbor. As the <u>France</u>, the former French liner maintained transatlantic service with the <u>QE2</u> in the early 1970s.

QE2

The Official Pictorial History

Produced for Cunard Line by

Sequoia Communications,
Santa Barbara, California.

Editor: Nicky Leach
Contributing Editor: Jamie Ellis
Design: Nanette Boyer
Type: Graphic Traffic, Santa Barbara

Printed in Hong Kong

ISBN: 0-917859-35-9

ACKNOWLEDGEMENTS

We are very grateful to the many people who have contributed to this book. Special thanks to George Donahue, Ron Santangelo, Susan Alpert, Wendy Sternberg, and Mike Smith at Cunard Line for their assistance. The author also wishes to thank Frank Braynard, Richard Tenney, and William Sauder for their help with editorial and illustration work.

ILLUSTRATION CREDITS

AUTHOR'S COLLECTION: 8, 15, 16 (left and bottom right), 24 (top), 25, 32-33, 50, 51; *SCOTT J. BECKER:* 49 (bottom), 56-57; *CENTRAL PRESS PHOTOS:* 36 (bottom right) and Queen Mary Archives; *ROBERT COATES:* 26 (left) and Queen Mary Archives; *CUNARD LINE:* flaps, 2-3, 6, 9, 10, 11 (middle and bottom), 12 (top), 13, 14 (bottom), 15 (right), 16 (top and bottom), 17 (left), 21 (bottom), 24 (bottom), 26 (right) and Queen Mary Archives, 27 (bottom right), 28 (middle) and Queen Mary Archives, 29 (bottom), 35 (center), 38, 39, 40 and Queen Mary Archives, 42, 44 (right and lower left), 45, 49 (top), 53 (bottom left), 54 (bottom photos), 55 (top right and bottom left), 58, 59 (top left, middle, lower right, bottom left), 61 (bottom left), 63, 64; *DAILY EXPRESS:* 21 (top) and Queen Mary Archives; *EASTMAN KODAK:* inside front/p. 1; *GLASGOW EVENING HERALD:* 35 (bottom), 53 (bottom right) and Cunard; *JOHN W. GREGORY:* 17 (right); *IMPERIAL WAR MUSEUM, LONDON:* 21 (middle); *LONDON TIMES:* 27 (bottom left) and Queen Mary Archives; *MAN B&W:* 52 (top and bottom right); *KEN MARSCHALL:* 14 (top) collection of Joseph Ryan, 52 (bottom left); *PETER MALINOWSKI:* 39, 59 (bottom right), 60, 61 (top, middle, bottom right), 62; *OCEAN PICTURES:* 28 (bottom) and Queen Mary Archives; *QUEEN MARY ARCHIVES:* 5, 11 (top), 12 (middle and bottom), 18, 19 (bottom), 20, 22, 23, 26 (bottom), 28 (top), 29 (top), 34, 35 (top left), 36 (top left and right, bottom left), 44 (top), 53 (top right); *RADIO TIMES:* 27 (top) and Queen Mary Archives; *MIKE RALPH:* 47, 48; *SCOTTISH DAILY RECORD:* 19 (top) and Queen Mary Archives; *JOHN SHAUM:* 43, 46; *ROBERT TWEEDIE:* 31.

Every effort has been made to verify facts, descriptions, and historic references in this book. Any omissions or misattributions are unintentional.

Table of Contents

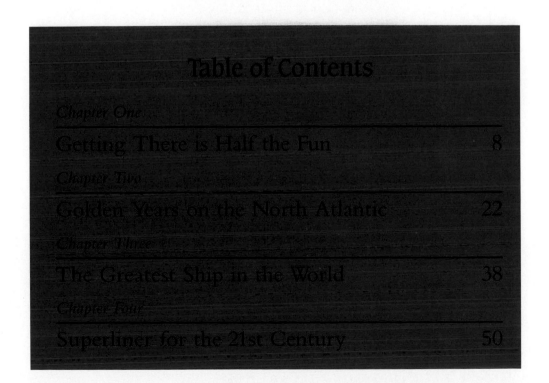

Britannia 1840   1,135 tons

Persia 1856   3,300 tons

CUNARD
125th ANNIVERSARY
1840~1965

Bothnia 1874   4,535 tons

Campania 1893   12,950 tons

Mauretania 1907   31,938 tons

Queen Mary 80,774 tons

Queen Elizabeth 83,678 tons

Carmania 22,600 tons

Chapter One

Getting There
is Half the Fun

Samuel Cunard began his steamship company with a vision, but it is unlikely that he could have foreseen a ship with the size, speed, or even purpose of the *Queen Elizabeth 2*. His original steamships were built simply to provide a transportation service for passengers and mail, often with the barest of amenities. The *Queen Elizabeth 2* was conceived to be a luxury liner, sailing around the world as well as on a traditional Atlantic sea route.

In 1824, Samuel Cunard foresaw a profitable steamship service carrying the mail from Halifax, Nova Scotia, to Boston and Bermuda, and was subsequently awarded a subsidy from the British government to develop the venture.

In 1831, Cunard invested in a small 176-foot steamship, the *Royal William,* which became the second steamship to cross the Atlantic Ocean, making the trip in 20 days. She carried 330 tons of coal, a box of stuffed birds, one box, seven trunks, a quantity of household furniture, and one harp. Each of her seven passengers paid £20.

In 1838, the British admiralty called for the construction of three steamships of not less than 300 tons to maintain a monthly transatlantic mail service.

Samuel Cunard won the contract, which provided an annual sum of £55,000, but he needed to find a financial backer and someone to build his ships. He was recommended to Robert Napier, a renowned marine engineer located on the Clyde River in Scotland. Financial backing was provided by Cunard and Napier, along with Glasgow ship-owners George Burns and David MacIver.

The contract was formally signed by the British admiralty and the newly-formed British and North American Royal Mail Steam Packet Company on May 4, 1839. However, it was soon realized that in order to fulfill the contract's monthly schedule, four ships, not three, would be required. The admiralty consented to the new proposal, increasing the annual subsidy from £55,000 to £60,000.

July 4 not only celebrates the historic date of independence of the United States, but also marks the anniversary of the maiden voyage of Cunard's first ship, the *Britannia.* She left Liverpool, England, on July 4, 1840, arriving in Halifax 12 days, 10 hours later, finishing the crossing in Boston on July 18. Her arrival was heralded with gun salutes and a civic banquet. Samuel Cunard, himself a passenger on the maiden voyage, received no less than 1,873 dinner invitations and a 30-inch-high silver loving cup, paid for by 2,500 citizens of Boston. The cup now occupies an honored place in the *Queen Elizabeth 2's* Columbia Restaurant.

The *Britannia* and her sister ships, *Acadia, Caledonia* and *Columbia,* were each 1,154 gross tons, 207 feet in length, driven by paddle wheels providing a service speed of nine knots (10.35 miles per hour). The success of these four ships led to larger and faster ocean liners. Cunard remained at the forefront of marine technology, building the sister

LEFT: A special commemorative menu cover celebrating Cunard Line's 125th anniversary.
BELOW: The silver loving cup given to Samuel Cunard by the citizens of Boston upon the maiden voyage arrival of the <u>Britannia</u>.

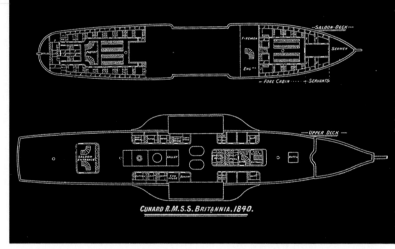

CUNARD R.M.S.S. BRITANNIA. 1840.

TOP: In February 1844, a seven-mile-long channel, paid for by Boston merchants, was cut through harbor ice to free the <u>Britannia</u> from possible destruction. MID-DLE: Blueprints of the <u>Britannia</u>. The interiors of the <u>Britannia</u> were far from lavish, as passenger Charles Dickens wrote from his cabin (BOTTOM RIGHT). An 1870s view of passengers on the deck of a ship (BOTTOM LEFT) failed to show the un-comfortable and sometimes haz-ardous conditions.

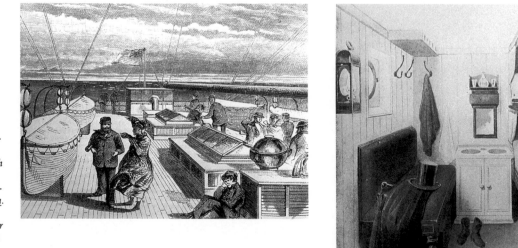

ships *Alps* and *Andes* in 1852: the first Cunarders with iron hulls and a propeller replacing the paddlewheels. The *Servia* was constructed in 1881, Cunard's first Atlantic mail service ship with a steel hull, and the first Cunarder to be lit by electricity.

The first Cunard ships with twin propellers were the *Campania* and *Lucania* of 1893. The *Lucania* became famous because of on-board experiments with wireless communication, conducted by its inventor, Guglielmo Marconi. Equipped with this brand new technology, the *Lucania* also became the first vessel to provide a ship's newspaper.

The *Carpathia*, constructed in 1903, played one of the most famous roles in maritime history. Steaming full speed between numerous icebergs, she answered the distress calls of the White Star liner *Titanic*, picking up all 705 survivors of the 1912 disaster.

TOP: The Cunard Line began a massive shipbuilding effort with the Servia in 1881. The Campania, with her revolutionary twin propellers (MIDDLE) won the Blue Riband for Cunard in 1893. BOTTOM: Past captains of Cunard ships.

Cunard's history-making ships: the Carpathia (TOP), commanded by Captain Arthur Rostron, came to the rescue of the Titanic; the Caronia (MIDDLE) and her sister ship Carmania, pioneered the use of large marine steam turbine engines; and the 12,950-ton Lucania (BOTTOM) supplied her passengers with the first daily news by wireless.

Following long negotiations, the British government agreed to lend the Cunard Line £2,600,000 for two new ships to compete with the high-speed German liners. In return, Cunard guaranteed that all of their ships would be available for government service in case of emergency.

In 1904, Cunard Line began to construct two almost identical ships of 650-foot length and 19,500 tons, the *Caronia* and *Carmania*. The *Caronia* was built with standard quadruple expansion reciprocating engines, while the *Carmania* had innovative steam turbine engines. The two ships were monitored closely, comparing their respective speeds, fuel economy, and most importantly, reliability. Cunard quickly realized that the marine steam turbine engine surpassed the traditional reciprocating engine in every category. Only after these in-service experiments were they satisfied with the decision to equip the new superliners with steam turbine engines.

The contract for construction of the first of Cunard's express liners, the *Lusitania,* was awarded to John Brown and Company in Clydebank, Scotland, while the second, the *Mauretania,* was to be built at Swan, Hunter and Wigham Richardson at Wallsend-on-Tyne. The *Lusitania* was launched first—the largest ship in the world at 31,550 gross tons. On her second westbound voyage in October 1907, she became the first ship to cross the Atlantic in under five days. She won back the symbolic Blue Riband for Britain with a crossing averaging 23.99 knots, and steamed back to her home port of Liverpool at a just slightly slower average speed of 23.61 knots.

Meanwhile the *Mauretania* was being fitted out at the Swan, Hunter yard, following her launch on September 20, 1906. To the untrained eye, the two sister ships seemed to be identical. Each was about 790 feet in length and 88 feet in width. The

The dimensions of the
Q. T. S. S. *Mauretania* are:
Length Overall - - 787 ft
Between Perpendicu-
lars, - - 760 ft
Beam, - - 88 ft.
Depth, - 60 ft. 6 in.
Gross Tonnage. - 33,200.
Maximum Draught. 37 ft.
corresponding to a Dis-
placement of 43,000 tons.
The I, H, P, of her Turbines
being 68,000, she can travel
27 knots per hour,

(QUADRUPLE-TURBINE) S.S. MAURETANIA
THE LARGEST VESSEL AFLOAT.

The Mauretania *was a well-loved ship, with magnificent interiors, such as her First Class Dining Saloon (TOP AND BOTTOM RIGHT). She gallantly served as a troopship during World War I in her "dazzle paint" (BOTTOM LEFT), designed to fool enemy shipping.*

Mauretania was actually slightly larger, measuring 488 tons more than the *Lusitania*.

The *Mauretania* departed Liverpool and Queenstown on November 16, 1907, on her maiden voyage to New York. On her first return crossing, she broke the *Lusitania's* eastbound record, steaming from New York to Queenstown in 5 days, 10 hours and 50 minutes, averaging 23.69 knots. The remarkable power of the *Mauretania's* turbine engines was proven as she arrived in Queenstown before the White Star liner *Baltic,*

which had left New York two days ahead of her.

Cunard's two ships ran with extreme efficiency, not only using less coal than was originally estimated, but as the ships were "broken in," they continued to beat each other's speed records. The *Mauretania* became known as the "Atlantic Greyhound" for her fast and extremely consistent voyages.

The sinking of the White Star liner *Titanic* had a significant effect on all of the transatlantic ships. The *Lusitania* and *Mauretania* increased their 16

Following the sinking of the White Star liner Titanic, dramatically depicted in this painting by Ken Marschall, a special medal (BOTTOM LEFT) was minted for the crew of the Cunard liner Carpathia for her role in the rescue of the Titanic's 705 survivors.

lifeboats to 48, while a third Cunard express liner, the *Aquitania,* was being constructed with high standards in watertight subdivision and equipped with a total of 80 lifeboats.

Her 901-foot hull was launched at John Brown Shipyard on April 21, 1913. At 45,646 gross tons, she was substantially larger than her two running mates, but not as fast. Together they were to form Cunard's weekly transatlantic passenger and mail service, but the *Aquitania* made only three voyages before World War I was declared. "The Ship Beautiful" was fitted out as an armed merchant cruiser, but this duty was soon judged unworkable. The guns were removed, and the *Aquitania* was converted into a troop transport, later also serving as a hospital ship.

The *Mauretania* was withdrawn from transatlantic service for several months, and like the *Aquitania* was converted to transport troops and wounded personnel. The *Lusitania* continued her normal transatlantic travel, however, beginning in November 1914, sailing only once a month because of the lack of passenger traffic. To keep losses at a minimum, she steamed with six of her 25 boilers shut down, which slowed her cruising speed by five knots, but let her remain the fastest ship on the Atlantic.

The early months of 1915 were filled with threats of war, and the German consulates in the United States issued clear warnings to citizens of still-neutral countries who wished to travel on ships of nations that were at war with Germany.

These warnings proved to be more than threats when the *Lusitania* was torpedoed by the German submarine U-20 on May 7, 1915. She was sailing with a secret cargo of ammunition just a few miles from her docking in Liverpool, when she was hit by a single torpedo, and went down in 18 minutes with the loss of 1,198 persons, including 124 Americans.

The *Mauretania* and *Aquitania* continued their valiant transport service through the balance of World War I, carrying a total of 130,000 personnel. The *Aquitania* saw temporary peacetime service for four months until it was decided that she should undergo a complete overhaul, including the conversion of her boilers to burn oil instead of coal.

The *Aquitania* returned to service on July 17, 1920, running with the *Mauretania* and *Berengaria*. The latter was formerly the German liner *Imperator,* which had been awarded to Cunard as compensation for the loss of the *Lusitania*. While berthed in Southampton on June 25, 1921, the *Mauretania* nearly met with tragedy. A workman cleaning carpets with an inflammable solvent accidentally started a fire which quickly spread to all of the

The Lusitania traded speed records with the Mauretania until her untimely sinking. The Lusitania's splendid First Class Lounge (RIGHT) was one of the most beautiful rooms afloat. BOTTOM: Interior of the Berengaria.

TOP: The __Aquitania__ was called "The Ship Beautiful" for her classic hull and superstructure lines. Her interiors, such as the Cabin Dining Salon (MID-DLE), were lavishly outfitted. During World War I, the __Aquitania__ took on the white hull and green stripes of a hospital ship (BOTTOM).

cabins on Main Deck, and threatened to extend to the rest of the ship through the First Class Dining Room above.

Perhaps even more dangerous than the fire was the amount of water which was being poured onto the upper decks. As the weight of the water increased, a mooring line snapped, immediately producing a 15-degree list to the starboard side. This caused the water to flood to that side, where all of the steel shell doors in the hull were closed. Through the heroic efforts of Senior First Officer James Bisset (later a captain of both *Queen* liners) and a group of volunteers, the hull doors were opened, allowing the water to drain off the ship.

The damage from the fire prompted the

Mauretania to undergo her long-delayed post-war overhaul. Her engines were converted to burn oil, making the 15-year-old record-holding ship even faster. Passenger traffic on the North Atlantic fell 25 percent between 1926 and 1931, but construction of new superliners continued in full swing. A 15-year interval with no large ship construction followed the *Aquitania*'s maiden voyage, but the next seven years saw the emergence of six huge liners, five of them record-holders. These were Germany's *Bremen* and *Europa*, Italy's *Rex* and *Conte di Savoia*, the French Line's *Normandie*, and Cunard's first 1000-foot superliner, the *Queen Mary*.

Samuel Cunard

Surprisingly, the founder of England's most famous steamship line was a Canadian, born in 1787 in Halifax, Nova Scotia, to Abraham and Irisa Cunard.

Ships were an important part of young Samuel's life from an early age as his father was a master carpenter in the busy port of Halifax. When Samuel was old enough, Abraham secured a job for his son as an engineer in a dockside lumberyard.

In 1808, at the age of 21, Samuel Cunard and his father formed their own ship chandlering firm of Abraham Cunard & Son, which sold provisions to ships. A year later, the *Savannah* became the first steamship to cross the Atlantic, despite using sails for all but eight hours of the voyage. This historic event would eventually pave the way for a new faster shipping service across the Atlantic. And Samuel Cunard would play an important part in it.

In 1812, young Cunard secured the right from the governor of Nova Scotia to begin trading with ports in the United States. In 1824, just after Abraham Cunard's retirement, the British admiralty awarded Samuel Cunard the contract to carry the mail between Halifax, Newfoundland, Boston, and Bermuda.

Samuel Cunard was now a respected name in the Halifax shipping business. He owned sailing ships, warehouses, and wharves, and was involved in the whaling trade. He also found time to be the city's fire warden, a colonel in the Halifax Militia, and elected to the elite Council of Twelve in the Nova Scotian legisla-ture. However, his life of success and fortune was hit by tragedy in 1828, when Susan, Cunard's wife of 12 years, died following the birth of their ninth child.

Although extremely successful, Cunard was known to be quite conservative. When approached in 1829 to support a steamship service between Halifax and Quebec, he declared, "We are entirely unacquainted with the cost of a steamboat, and would not like to embark in a business of which we are quite ignorant." He changed his mind, however, following a ride on George Stephenson's "Rocket" railway during a trip to England. On his return to Halifax, he predicted that, "Steamers properly built and manned might start and arrive at their destination with the punctuality of rail-road trains on land."

In 1831, Samuel and his brothers, Henry and Joseph, invested in the steamship *Royal William,* servicing Halifax and Quebec. Two years later, the tiny 364-ton steamship crossed the Atlantic with seven passengers. The *Royal William* was claimed to be the first to make the entire trip entirely under steam power, although her captain admitted that every fourth day her engines were shut down between 24 and 26 hours to clear the boilers of salt deposits.

An advertisement appearing in the November 8, 1838 issue of the London *Times* led to the formation of Cunard's first steamship company. It read,"Steam vessels required for conveying Her Majesty's mails and dispatches between England and Halifax, Nova Scotia, and also between England, Halifax, and New York." Tenders were to be submitted to the admiralty before December 15, 1838, but Cunard did not receive the paper until after the dead-line had passed.

He sailed immediately for Falmouth, England, to make his successful proposal, resulting in the construction of the *Britannia* and her sister ships, *Acadia, Caledonia,* and *Columbia.*

In recognition of his accomplishments, Samuel Cunard was made a baron by Queen Victoria in 1859. He died at his London home in 1865, having seen his steamship company become the most prestigious on the Atlantic.

With Samuel Cunard's backing, the steamship Royal William *crossed the Atlantic in 1833, powered by two 80-horsepower engines.*

"THE INEVITABLE SHIP"

Designs for Cunard Line's first 1000-foot liner began in 1926, as long-term replacements for the *Mauretania* and *Aquitania* were going to be needed. Plans called for construction of two huge liners; the rapid increase in marine technology now allowed two ships to do the job previously requiring three. Sir Percy Bates, the chairman of Cunard Line between 1930 and 1946, said it best when he announced, "The Cunard Company is projecting a pair of steamers which though they will be very large and fast, are, in fact, the smallest and slowest which can fulfill properly all essential economic conditions." In other words, the *Queen Mary* had to measure 1,019.5 feet long, 118 feet wide, and 81,237 gross tons, in order to carry enough passengers to pay for operation of steam turbine engines, powerful enough to maintain a 28.5-knot cruising speed. This would allow the *Queen Mary* and her forthcoming sister ship, the *Queen Elizabeth,* to provide a weekly passenger and mail service between the continents.

The keel was laid for Job #534 on December 1, 1930, at John Brown Shipyard. Work continued at a steady pace for almost a year. The Great Depression, which was hitting Britain, caused the banks providing money to Cunard for construction of the ship to suddenly stop issuing loans. Without the money to continue, construction of the ship completely halted on December 10, 1931. Over 3,000 men at Clydebank were put out of work, plus up to 10,000 more in other parts of Great Britain. The *Daily Telegraph* described it as an "industrial catastrophe."

In France, the French Line was building a 1000-foot liner of its own at Penhoet Shipyard, St. Nazaire. The *Normandie*'s construction was never hampered, thanks to loans provided by the French government. Cunard Line wanted this same privilege from the British Parliament. Percy Bates, along with Clydebank M.P. David Kirkwood and Neville Chamberlain, fought a two-year battle for funds to continue construction. Kirkwood pleaded before the British House of Commons, "I believe that as long as this ship, known as 534, lies like a skeleton in my constituency, so long will depression last in this country....It seems to me to shout 'failure, failure' to the whole of Britain."

Finally, an agreement was hammered out. In order to strengthen Britain's shipping industry, the government passed the North Atlantic Shipping Bill, lending £9.5 million to Cunard and White Star Line, with the condition that the two rival British lines merge.

Two years and four months after work on the *Queen Mary* had been suspended, the men of Clydebank marched back to work. She was quickly readied for launch, scheduled in late 1934. In keeping with Cunard Line's tradition of christening its ships with names ending in "ia", they decided to name Job #534, *Queen Victoria*. A delegation from Cunard called on King George V, to ask his permission. Sir Ashley Sparks, chairman of Cunard in America, told the King that Cunard wished to name its new ship after

"England's greatest queen." Queen Mary, who was with her husband, smiled and said, "I would be delighted."

On the day of the launch—September 26, 1934—the name of Job #534 was still a secret. King George gave a superb speech, coining the title of "the stateliest ship," which would stay with the *Queen Mary* until today. Her Majesty Queen Mary stepped to the microphone and announced, "I am happy to name this ship the *Queen Mary*." A great roar came from the 200,000 persons gathered, then the Queen pushed the button releasing the six hydraulic triggers holding the ship in place. As the *Queen Mary* slid into the Clyde River, 2,300 tons of drag chains slowed her momentum and soon a swarm of tugboats took control and pushed the ship into her fitting-out basin.

The same day in September which saw the beginning of the *Queen Mary's* career saw the end of another era. The beloved *Mauretania* departed New York for the last time, to be tied up at Berth 108, the death row for ocean liners in Southampton. The construction of the *Queen Mary,* and later the *Queen Elizabeth,* signaled the end of her career, as well as seven White Star ships, including the *Olympic, Majestic, Homeric, Doric,* and *Albertic.* The *Aquitania* was also due to be scrapped, but her World War II service extended her years at sea.

Following the launch of the *Queen Mary,* an additional 20 months were required to install over 26,000 tons of equipment, including her luxurious interior appointments, propulsion machinery and superstructure, topped by her three famous Cunard red and black funnels. On March 24, 1936, the *Queen Mary* began her journey down the Clyde River to the open sea. Despite elaborate precautions taken to dredge

and widen the river, she still managed to run aground at the notorious Double Beardmore Bend. No damage was apparent, but the *Queen Mary* was recorded on Lloyd's list of wrecks on the very first day under her own power.

The *Queen Mary's* maiden voyage begun on May 27, 1936, was one of great anticipation of capturing the Atlantic speed record, won by the French Line's *Normandie* on her own maiden voyage a year earlier. The challenger departed Southampton, then after her normal short stop in Cherbourg, France, raced past the traditional landmark for the start of the Blue Riband crossing, Bishop's Rock.

Fog encountered on the third day at sea prevented the *Queen Mary* from taking the record on her first crossing, but despite the delay, the liner arrived in New York with a new one-day's distance record of 766 nautical miles, and came within minutes of the *Normandie's* record crossing. Cunard Line had endured great pressure for the *Queen Mary* to win the Blue Riband, now in the form of a trophy commissioned by British M.P. Harold Hales. Cunard consistently denied trying to beat the record, attributing the *Queen Mary's* high speed to research for design of her sister ship. However, Commodore Britten was asked by the press upon the ship's arrival in New York whether he thought the *Queen Mary* could win the trophy on a future voyage. He exclaimed, "Well naturally . . . what have we built her for!"

The *Queen Mary* did win the Blue Riband back for Britain in August 1936, and after the *Normandie* had made a quicker voyage, steamed even faster a year later. She kept the record for 14 years until the liner *United States* smashed it in 1952, but Cunard Line kept to its conviction and never formally accepted the Hales Trophy.

LEFT: The Queen Mary *is nudged into her New York berth by the tugboat* Alice M. Moran. *TOP: Spectators line the banks of the Clyde River to wish the new superliner* Queen Mary *good luck on her way to the sea. BOTTOM RIGHT: Cunard Line never accepted British M.P. Harold Hales' trophy for the winner of the Blue Riband, despite the image of the* Queen Mary *on the trophy.*

CONSTRUCTION OF A SISTER SHIP

The *Queen Elizabeth* began as Job #552 at John Brown Shipyard on December 4, 1936. Her design incorporated many improvements over the *Queen Mary*. Because of progress in marine technology, the *Queen Elizabeth* needed only 12 boilers instead of 27, meaning only two funnels were necessary. The huge boiler room ventilators, prominent on the *Queen Mary's* upper decks, were eliminated, allowing even more passenger deck space. A sleeker look forward on the *Queen Elizabeth* was provided by the absence of a sunken "well deck." The addition of a third anchor also required more rake, or slope, to her bow.

The construction of the hull of the *Queen Elizabeth* went smoothly, without the complications and delays suffered by the *Queen Mary*. The launch on September 27, 1938, by Her Majesty Queen Elizabeth took much the same form as that performed by her mother-in-law, Queen Mary, four years earlier. King George VI had planned to attend as well, but because of the gathering threats of war in Europe had to cancel at the last minute. The Queen herself made the launching speech, stating, "The launching of a ship is like the inception of all great human enterprises, an act of faith. We proclaim our belief that by the Grace of God, and by man's patience and good will, order may yet be brought out of confusion and peace out of turmoil. With that hope and prayer in our hearts we send forth upon her mission this noble ship."

Following her official naming and launch into the Clyde River, she was moved into the fitting-out basin for completion. As the threat of war continued to mount, there was increasing concern over her presence in the shipyard, not only as a prime target for German bombers, but taking up valuable shipyard space and materials which could be used for wartime needs. The decision was made in September 1939 to complete only essential construction. Only two days each year were available to move the *Queen Elizabeth* from the shipyard because of tidal conditions, so the ship was quickly made ready to sail on the first date, February 26, 1940. The battleship *Duke of York* was scheduled to take the *Queen Elizabeth's* place, but if the operation did not go as planned, the liner would be stranded there for six months.

While the *Queen Elizabeth* was preparing for her first voyage, the *Queen Mary* was continuing her transatlantic service, carrying more and more passengers fleeing Europe. Her last westbound crossing in August 1939, she carried a record 2,329 passengers including Bob Hope and J.P. Morgan. At the end of the crossing, she was detained at Cunard Line's New York pier in the comparative safety of the still-neutral United States. The German U-Boats made continuing her North Atlantic service too hazardous, and there were no safe locations for her to be berthed in Great Britain. The French Line pier in New York held the *Normandie,* also in the same situation.

Secret meetings held by Cunard Line officials concluded that the *Queen Elizabeth* should also go to New York. Her new Cunard red, black, and white paint was covered with camouflage grey. Elaborate plans were made to deceive the Germans about her destination, and word was spread that she would proceed to Southampton for routine drydocking and preparation for sea trials. The huge King George V drydock was prepared for her arrival, supplies were sent to Southampton, and 400 crew members were signed on for the three-day voyage.

The *Queen Elizabeth* made the 15-mile journey down the Clyde River without mishap. Once at anchor at Tail of the Bank, she was officially handed over to Cunard Line without the normal

The Queen Mary, the Queen Elizabeth, and the Normandie at berth in New York harbor. The original caption reads, "At rest for the rest of the war," but history would prove otherwise in the Queen liners' troopship duty during World War II, and the tragic loss of the Normandie.

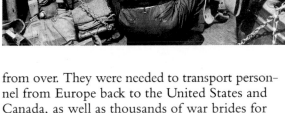

exhaustive tests or trials. Finally the crew could be told that they were not proceeding to Southampton. Only after her departure on the morning of March 2 did Captain Jack Townley learn by sealed envelope delivered by the King's messenger that he was to take the *Queen Elizabeth* to New York. The false rumors of the ship steaming to Southampton proved to be an excellent lure. A large force of German bombers was waiting over the English Channel at the time of her anticipated arrival.

Five days and nine hours after leaving Britain, the *Queen Elizabeth* was spotted zig-zagging furiously as she approached New York. She tied up at Pier 90, and for the only time in history, three 1,000-foot superliners were berthed together on Manhattan's West Side. Two weeks later, the *Queen Mary* departed for Singapore by way of Cape Town, South Africa, to be drydocked and re-fitted to carry over 5,000 troops. She began her wartime service carrying Australian and New Zealand troops to the Suez. In November 1940, the *Queen Elizabeth* departed New York for Singapore to undergo similar conversion. She joined her sistership as part of the "Indian Ocean Shuttle" in April 1941.

When the South Pacific became too hazardous for the liners, they were transferred to the North Atlantic, transporting American and Canadian troops to Europe. By late 1942, the *Queens* had their carrying capacities raised, topping 15,000 troops during the summer months. The *Queen Mary* still holds the record for "the greatest number of souls on a floating vessel" with 16,683 persons carried between New York and Gourock, Scotland, in July 1943.

Peace was declared in Europe in May 1945, but the wartime work of the Cunard ships was far from over. They were needed to transport personnel from Europe back to the United States and Canada, as well as thousands of war brides for reunions with their husbands and fiances.

Cunard Line had played a huge role in determining the outcome of World War II. The sheer speed and size of the two *Queen* liners made possible rapid transportation of entire divisions of troops in relative safety. Sir Percy Bates, Chairman of Cunard, remarked, "I would like to think the two ships (*Queen Mary* and *Queen Elizabeth*) shortened the war by one year."

Sir Winston Churchill observed, "Built for the arts of peace and to link the old world with the new, the *Queens* challenged the fury of Hitlerism… to defend the liberties of civilization. Vital decisions depended on their ability continuously to elude the enemy, and without their aid, the day of final victory must unquestionably have been postponed." In a fitting tribute to the men of John Brown Shipyard, he said, "To those who brought these two great ships into existence, the world owes a debt that will not be easy to measure."

The Queen Elizabeth is seen loading 15,000 American airmen in Southampton, England, for the journey home in August 1945. Living conditions on both Queen liners were crowded during World War II. Soldiers aboard the Queen Mary (CENTER) spend their time playing cards while crossing the Atlantic. BOTTOM: Queen Elizabeth interior.

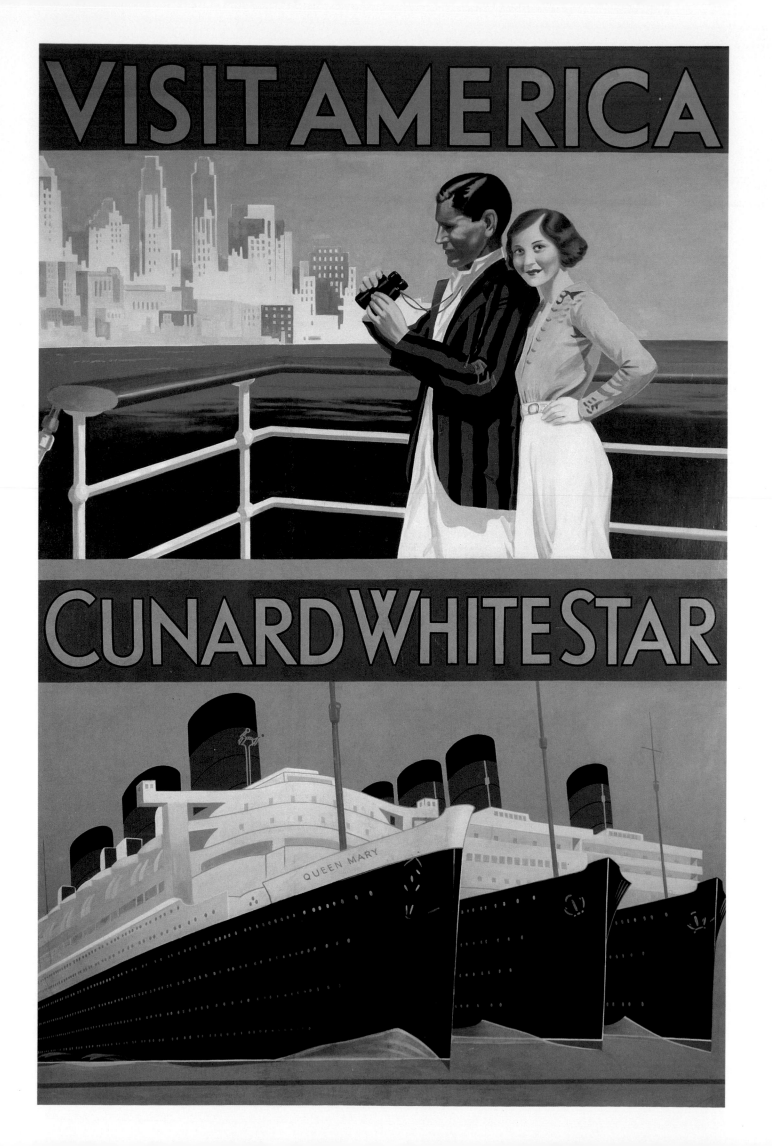

Chapter Two

Golden Years on the North Atlantic

T he *Queen Elizabeth* was the first Cunard ship discharged from her troopship duties to be transformed from Her Majesty's Transport to her intended role as the *Royal Mail Ship Queen Elizabeth.* A period of seven months was needed to track down all of the liner's fittings from around the world and ship them back to Southampton for reinstallation.

The *Queen Mary* was returned to Cunard in September 1946, along with the second *Mauretania,* which had been completed just before the war. The *Aquitania* made 25 special voyages to Canada after the war, carrying emigrants as well as returning troops from Europe. With both *Queen* liners in service, Cunard announced withdrawal of the *Aquitania* in 1949, ending her last Atlantic voyage in Southampton on December 1.

The *Queen Elizabeth* had sailed over 492,000 miles and had carried 811,000 personnel during World War II, but now transformed, she was a symbol of Britain's recovery. Her furniture and luxurious fittings had been carefully stored during the war, but perishable supplies for her first series of voyages, not available in Britain, were specially shipped from America on the *Aquitania.* Her maiden voyage on October 16, 1946, was filled with emotion as the people of Southampton turned out by the thousands to wish the *Queen Elizabeth* good luck.

Action in World War II had eliminated much of Cunard Line's competition on the Atlantic, but the incident which was perhaps the most tragic was the loss of the *Normandie* in New York. The huge liner was laid up in 1939 at the French Line pier, and seized by the United States government in 1941. The *Normandie* was renamed the *U.S.S. Lafayette,* and work was begun to convert her into a troop transport ship. On February 9, 1942, a group of welders accidentally set fire to a stack of flammable kapok life jackets. The fire spread quickly and after 12 hours of fire fighting, enough water had been poured onto the *Normandie's* upper decks to capsize her at the pier. In an unprecedented salvage operation taking 20 months and $5 million, the *Normandie* was righted and eventually sold to a scrap yard for $161,000.

The return to peace prompted Cunard Line to order a new 34,000-ton liner from John Brown Shipyard. Named after the *Caronia* of 1904, the ship's purpose was not to travel the North Atlantic, but to cruise to exotic ports in the Caribbean, Mediterranean, South Pacific, and Scandinavia. For this special purpose, her hull was painted light green and she become affectionately known as *"The Green Goddess."* The *Caronia* was Cunard's first ship built primarily for cruising, and was the initial step toward the dual North Atlantic/cruise ship design of the *Queen Elizabeth 2.*

LEFT: Transatlantic and cruise travel continued to grow in popularity after World War II. BOTTOM RIGHT: The swimming pool aboard the Queen Mary.

C^{IE} G^{LE} TRANSATLANTIQUE · FRENCH LINE

"NORMANDIE" LE HAVRE · SOUTHAMPTON · NEW YORK

Intérieur du Gd Paquebot NORMANDIE. Le Fumoir des 1ères Classes.

TOP: The superliner Norman-die, along with the Queen Mary, carried the cream of the North Atlantic travelers during the late Thirties. MIDDLE: Interior of the Normandie. BOTTOM: Built for speed, the SS United States took the record for the fastest Atlantic crossing from the Queen Mary on her maiden voyage in 1952.

Post-war travel on the Atlantic was booming, and Cunard Line was obtaining a great share of the business. Seeing room for competition, the United States Line began work on its first superliner. They learned from the Queens' adaptability to troop-carrying service, but instead of designing a luxury liner which could be converted to a troop ship, they conceived a troop ship which would perform as a luxury liner.

Because of this prerequisite, the SS United States was a unique ship in many ways. Aluminum was used extensively for its light weight and fire-resistant properties. Unlike the 1,000-foot-long Queens, the 990-foot United States was designed to be able to travel through the Panama Canal. Her most impressive feature, however, was her 240,000 shaft horsepower, compared to the Queens' 160,000. Using that added power, the United States easily took the Blue Riband on her maiden voyage in July 1952, with an amazing average speed of 35.59 knots. The eastbound crossing was 10 hours faster than the Queen Mary's 14-year-old record.

In the mid-1950s, Cunard Line began replacing some of the ships that had provided service from Canada to Europe before World War II. As the new 21,000-ton Saxonia made her maiden voyage in June 1957, Cunard Line was startled by an alarming situation developing on the Atlantic. That year saw, for the first time, more travellers flying the Atlantic than going by ship. In fact, in 1957, over one million persons took to the air. By 1964, that number had grown to three and a half million. A new superliner was about to be ordered by Cunard Line, but would she be the right ship?

DESIGN FOR A NEW QUEEN

The *Queens* were beginning to age. By 1966, the *Queen Mary* would reach 30, and plans needed to begin to design her replacement. It was assumed the new liner, known as *Q3,* would be comparable in size, continuing to serve the Atlantic following the withdrawal of the *Queen Elizabeth.* The ship would share a schedule with the new super-liner *France* built by the French Line in 1961.

However, several members of Cunard's board of directors favored a smaller ship which would continue on the North Atlantic route during the summer months, and adapt to cruising during the rest of the year. This new proposal would be known as *Q4* and eventually become the *Queen Elizabeth 2.*

Once the decision had been made to build the *Q4,* Cunard Line set about acquiring a new loan agreement with the British government. The loan for £17.6 million toward the estimated total cost at that time of £22 million would be repaid over 25 years at 4.5 percent interest.

John Brown Shipyard in Clydebank was once again chosen for the construction of Cunard Line's latest superliner, designated Job #736. She would be built at the Number 4 Building Berth, on the same spot as the prior *Queens.* John Brown had submitted the lowest bid of £25,427,000, and the earliest delivery date of May 1968. A contract was signed on December 30, 1964.

Overall transatlantic ship traffic dropped 10 percent in 1964. This prompted Cunard to make changes to its ships still in service. The *Queen Elizabeth* was withdrawn from service for four months in early 1966 for a £1.5 million re-fit in order to adapt her for limited cruising. Full air-conditioning was installed, along with an outdoor lido pool. Similar improvements were made on the *Caronia,* and £6 million was spent on the renamed *Carmania* and *Franconia,* formerly the *Saxonia* and *Ivernia.* Many new ideas for *Q4* related to her cruising role were designed by Cunard's chief naval architect, Dan Wallace, and first tested on these two ships.

The hull of the second *Mauretania* was painted "cruising green" in late 1962, and given a warm weather itinerary, but she could not compete with newer ships built solely for cruising. She was laid up in November 1965, and soon dispatched to the scrap yard.

In mid-1965, a huge 180-ton steel keel section, 117 feet long, 23 feet wide, and 6 feet high, was made ready to become the initial construction segment of Job #736. The piece was all-welded, radically different from the riveted construction of Cunard's previous superliners. The ceremonial laying of the keel was to take place on July 2, but when the time came for the section to be moved into position, the lifting tackle began to slip under the strain. The attempt was postponed several days, and accomplished without fanfare.

TOP: The Queen Elizabeth *in port. BOTTOM: Queen Elizabeth's personal standard.*

TOP RIGHT: The Queen Elizabeth was not able to enter passenger service until 1946. Fixtures for rooms such as her Second Class Lido Bar (ABOVE) and First Class Dining Room (BOTTOM) were kept in storage until the end of the war.

As the ship's designs became more firm, staggering statistics were revealed to an anxious British public. Job #736 would be the largest twin propeller ship ever built growing from an estimated 58,000 to 65,863 gross registered tons. The hull measured 963 feet long and 105 feet, 2.5 inches wide. Those inches became very important as this *Queen* liner would have to be able to fit through the 110-foot-wide locks of the Panama Canal. The *Mary* and *Elizabeth* were both too long and too wide to make the passage.

Advances in shipbuilding technology allowed John Brown to save 2,000 tons of weight in the ship's hull by welding, rather than using overlapping riveted steel plating. The superstructure is fabricated from aluminum, because of its light weight, corrosion resistance, and successful use on liners such as the *United States*.

Behind the scenes, Cunard Line's architects and engineers worked quietly on the design of the *Q4*. She had to be conceived with adaptations and compromises in order to be able to both "cross and cruise." For the Atlantic the ship needed to be fast, but economical at slower speeds for cruising. Steaming on the often-frigid North Atlantic required weather-protected passenger space, while cruising demanded as much open outdoor space as possible. Flexibility was the key word for the *Q4*.

Meanwhile, passenger traffic on the Atlantic in 1965 went from bad to worse. Despite a profit in Cunard Line's cargo ship operations, the company's passenger ships lost £2.7 million. A strike of British seamen began on May 16, 1966, lasting until July 1, during which Cunard's entire passenger ship fleet was shut down, costing an estimated £4 million. That year, Cunard lost a staggering total of £7.5 million.

Perhaps the most devastating event in 1966 was the announcement from John Brown Shipyard that the delivery of Job #736 would be delayed five months until November 1968. The shipyard was in financial difficulty, but this also meant Cunard would lose about £200,000 profit each week.

Effects of the British seamen's strike continued into 1967. On May 8, the captains of the *Queen Mary* and *Queen Elizabeth* opened sealed messages from the company, announcing the end of an era: the two liners would be withdrawn from service. Cunard had planned to retire the *Queen Mary* in late 1968 with the arrival of the *Q4,* and with her recent renovations, the *Queen Elizabeth* had been scheduled to remain in service until 1975 as the *Q4*'s running mate. Instead, the announcement spelled out a plan to withdraw the *Queen Mary* in October 1967, with the *Queen Elizabeth* to follow in late 1968. For Cunard Line to stay financially afloat there was no other choice, as the two ships were each losing £750,000 annually. The *Caronia* was sold for £1.25 million in November 1967, quickly followed a month later by the *Carinthia,* and the *Sylvania* in May 1968.

The *Queen Mary* was purchased by the city of Long Beach, California, for $3,450,000. She made her 500th and last round-trip transatlantic voyage to New York, arriving back in Southampton on September 26. The *Queen Mary* departed Southampton for the last time on October 31, for a historic 39-day voyage which took the ship and her 1,100 passengers across the Equator

TOP: The *Queen Mary* enters the massive King George V Graving Dock in Southampton, specially built for Cunard's two *Queen* liners. BOTTOM: Sailors from the aircraft carrier *H.M.S. Hermes* give the *Queen Mary* a salute at the beginning of her final voyage to Long Beach, California.

TOP: Despite going aground in the Clyde River on her first voyage to the sea, the Queen Mary went on to have an outstanding 31 years of service. The Queen Mary's First Class Pool (MIDDLE) is an art-deco masterpiece. BOTTOM: A final mid-Atlantic salute is given to the ship from the captain of the Queen Elizabeth.

twice and around the tip of South America. It was a difficult voyage, as the ship had to travel much longer distances between ports than on the Atlantic, saving fuel by operating only two of her four engines.

The *Queen Mary*'s reception in Long Beach on December 9, surpassed even her maiden voyage arrival in New York, 31 years earlier. An estimated 10,000 boats greeted her, along with up to a million persons on shore. Following four years of conversion work, the *Queen Mary* became a first class hotel, convention facility, and attraction. She still floats with the tides and can be admired by a whole new generation of "passengers."

Meanwhile in Clydebank, huge prefabricated steel and aluminum sections were being fitted to the ever-growing hull of the *Q4*. One last major announcement came from Cunard Line. Substantial increases in expenses caused John Brown Shipyard to revise their final cost, forcing Cunard to return to the British government for a new loan

agreement. The ship would cost an additional £3 million, raising the total price to £28.5 million. Just one week before Her Majesty Queen Elizabeth II was scheduled to launch *Q4*, Cunard Line and the British government agreed to increase the amount of its loan by £6.4 million to £24 million.

Upon the Queen Mary's arrival in Long Beach, California, Captain John Treasure Jones described his radar as being a solid blip due to the number of ships on hand to welcome the Queen Mary.

The Q3 Project

North Atlantic steamship travel was pioneered by the Cunard Line, so when planning for replacement of the *Queen Mary* and *Queen Elizabeth* was begun in the late 1950s, efforts were directed towards building two similar huge liners. The first new ship conceived by Cunard, designated *Q3,* would travel the Atlantic year-round like the previous *Queens.* The British government set up the independent Chandos Committee to advise Cunard on the best way to finance the replacement liner. Their recommendation was for the government to loan Cunard £18,000,000 toward a total cost not to exceed £30,000,000. The ship would be owned and operated by Cunard through a separate company.

Tenders for the construction of *Q3* were solicited in March 1961, and it was anticipated that an order for the ship would be placed by autumn at the latest. The lowest tender of £28 million came from a consortium of the well-known shipbuilding firms of Vickers Armstrong Ltd. and Swan, Hunter and Wigham Richardson.

The original plans for *Q3* showed a traditional hull and superstructure design with partially open promenade decks. The ship had a conventional funnel, but the mast also was to be used for smoke emission. A builder's model, shown several months later, revealed an enclosed promenade area, a whaleback type foredeck similar to the *France,* and a slim funnel matching the mast. She would be capable of carrying 2,259 passengers.

The *Q3*'s gross tonnage was to be between 75,000 and 85,000 tons, her length 990 feet, and breadth 116 feet. Her engines would be comparable to the prior *Queens,* with steam turbine engines, supplying 200,000 shaft horsepower to four propellers. Eight boilers would be capable of producing 950 degree steam at 850 p.s.i. Also, like the *France,* she would have the potential of conversion to nuclear propulsion.

The *Q3* proposal had been spearheaded in the late 1950s by Cunard chairman Colonel Denis Bates. When he died in 1959, it was becoming clear that the North Atlantic ships were losing out to the airliners. The new chairman, Sir John Brocklebank, along with several members of Cunard's board of directors, were convinced that the *Q3* proposal would lead the company straight to bankruptcy. They proposed a dual-purpose ship which would be powerful enough to keep up the North Atlantic route during the still-profitable summer months, but versatile enough to cruise warm-weather areas during the rest of the year. Advances in marine technology allowed the desired speed for the Atlantic to be achieved in a smaller twin-propeller ship, reducing manpower and fuel requirements. This new proposal would come to be known as *Q4,* and eventually become the *Queen Elizabeth 2.*

The QE2.

THE QE2 IS LAUNCHED

The long anticipated day of launching arrived on September 20, 1967. What had been merely a huge steel structure built on land would enter the water, her natural element, for the first time. But the hull known as Job #736, or simply Q4, would have to be given a name. The British public became enthralled with what the new superliner would be called, just as they had 33 years earlier at the launch of the *Queen Mary*. Thousands of names were suggested, with the favorites including *Sir Winston Churchill, Queen Victoria, Britannia,* and even *Princess Margaret*. (The habitually wagering British public gave *Queen Elizabeth* only 14 to 1 odds). Just four persons, including the Queen and her private secretary, knew the name supposed to be announced to the 30,000 spectators assembled in the shipyard.

Her Majesty Queen Elizabeth II was handed a card, just minutes before she was to perform the christening, by John Brown's managing director John Rannie, which read, "I name this ship *Queen Elizabeth*." But when the Queen stepped to the microphone to launch the ship at 2:28 pm, she made a last-second change. The Queen announced to the crowd, "I name this ship *Queen Elizabeth the Second*. May God bless her and all who sail in her."

As the assembled crowd reacted to the Queen's announcement, she pushed the button releasing the hydraulic trigger mechanism, the last remaining supports holding the ship in place. Seventy long seconds passed before the *Queen Elizabeth 2* was seen to move. A voice from on board the ship was heard to shout in a Scottish brogue, "Give 'er a shove." In fact, those observing the equipment monitoring the ship's motion reported movement as soon as the Queen pushed the button. Once the 22,000-ton hull gained momentum, it achieved an incredible 22 miles per hour down the slipway, before being slowed and stopped by 1,400 tons of drag chains.

Once the excitement of the launch had subsided, the spectators wondered whether the Queen had in fact used her own name in christening the ship, as her mother and grandmother had done, or named Q4 in honor of the ship *Queen Elizabeth,* then still in service. Cunard Line spokesmen later explained that an Arabic "2" would be used to signify the ship as being a successor to the liner *Queen Elizabeth,* rather than Her Majesty's Roman numeral II. *Queen Elizabeth 2* was quickly shortened to *QE2,* even being used to form the ship's first official logo.

In a little-known event following the launch festivities, John Brown Shipyard presented Her Majesty the Queen with a small speedboat for

Her Majesty Queen Elizabeth II is pictured next to Cunard Line chairman Sir Basil Small-peice as she prepares to launch the QE2.

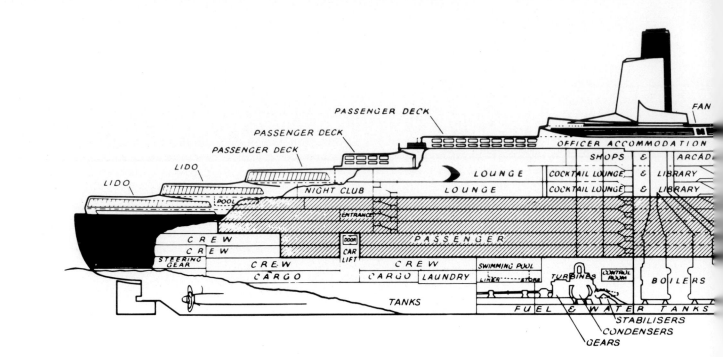

the Royal Yacht *Britannia*. The Queen expressed her thanks by saying, "I think we might appropriately call it John Brown and paint it in Cunard colors." A quick-witted listener, identified by some as Prince Philip, was heard to reply, "Why not call it Cunard and paint it brown?"

The Queen also made mention of the recent merger of John Brown Shipyard with a group of four other shipyards, to be known as Upper Clyde Shipbuilders. "The people who really deserve a toast today are the designers and builders of John Brown's latest great ship for the Cunard fleet," she remarked. "We have all read with a touch of nostalgia that the name of John Brown is to disappear from the list of great shipbuilders. However, this does not mean that the very special skill and spirit of this yard will be lost to Clydeside or to British shipbuilding."

Following the *Queen Elizabeth 2*'s successful launch, the work of installing her propelling machinery and luxurious interiors began. Thanks to advances in boiler technology, *Queen Elizabeth 2* would need only three boilers, as compared to the *Queen Mary*'s 27. Her turbine engines would be capable of producing a total of 110,000 shaft horsepower, and the on-board electrical generators were powerful enough to supply the needs of a city of 21,000. A fresh-water distillation plant was installed, able to produce over 250,000 gallons of water (approximately 9,600,000 glasses) every day. The world's smallest and most advanced computer at that time was used to monitor much of this machinery, including the fuel, fresh water, performance, and safety systems.

Cunard's design team was headed by their chief naval architect Dan Wallace. James Gardner and

Cunard liner "Queen Eliz

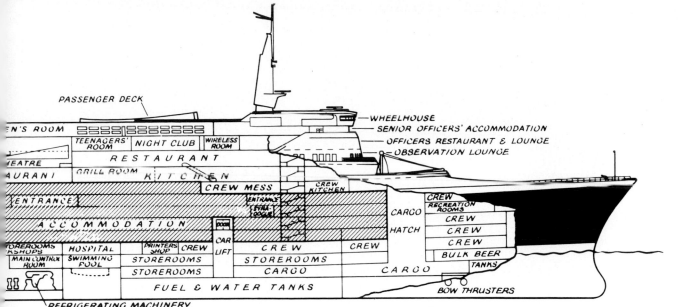

PASSENGER DECK

EN'S ROOM   WHEELHOUSE
TEENAGERS' ROOM   NIGHT CLUB   WIRELESS ROOM   SENIOR OFFICERS' ACCOMMODATION
THEATRE   RESTAURANT   OFFICERS RESTAURANT & LOUNGE
AURANT   GRILL ROOM   KITCHEN   OBSERVATION LOUNGE
CREW MESS   CREW KITCHEN
ENTRANCE   ENTRANCE   CARGO   CREW RECREATION ROOMS
ACCOMMODATION   DOOR   CAR LIFT   HATCH   CREW
STOREROOMS   HOSPITAL   PRINTERS SHOP   CREW   CREW   CREW   CREW
WORKSHOPS   SWIMMING POOL   STOREROOMS   STOREROOMS   BULK BEER
MAIN CONTROL ROOM   STOREROOMS   CARGO   CARGO   TANKS
FUEL & WATER TANKS   BOW THRUSTERS
REFRIGERATING MACHINERY
TURBO-ALTERNATORS
STABILISERS

and Dennis Lennon were hired as joint design coordinators. Gardner was responsible for the exterior design, including the superstructure, mast, and funnel, while Lennon was in charge of the liner's interior decoration.

The funnel design for the *Queen Elizabeth 2* is unique, and perhaps the most controversial aspect of the entire ship. A smokestack's location is determined by the location of the vessel's boilers. On the *QE2,* they are amidships. Twenty different funnel designs were tested in wind tunnels, under the supervision of James Gardner. In fast ships like *QE2,* smoke tends to swirl downward, and a traditional oval funnel proved to be unworkable. This led to a revolutionary design consisting of a relatively thin smokestack, 67 feet, 3 inches high, with a curved "scoop" at the base. This scoop directs airflow up, carrying the

smoke and gasses away from the decks. The single mast that holds radar equipment, as well as exhaust ventilators from the kitchens, along with the funnel, balances the look of the *QE2* for aesthetic appeal. This unique styling caused Gardner to abandon the historic Cunard red and black funnel colors, and employ white with a black smoke pipe and red scoop. However, following the Falkland Island battle, the traditional Cunard red funnel color with black top and striping was adopted for the ship.

Dennis Lennon's job was to take the restrictions of various hatches, ventilator trunks, and many other necessary obstructions, and design staterooms and public rooms around them that were both beautiful and functional. His designs always had to keep in mind the *QE2*'s dual "cross and cruise" role. The ship's original plans called for

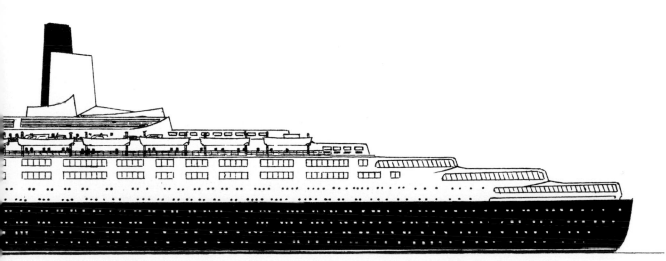

Drawing by J. H. Isherwood

commissioned January 1969

"QUEEN MARY" "QUEEN ELIZABETH"
Fastest Ocean Service in the World

CUNARD
WHITE STAR

687 standard staterooms, all with a bath or shower, plus 291 deluxe rooms including 46 luxury suites. Passengers would dine in three separate restaurants, and swim in two indoor and two outdoor pools.

The *Queen Elizabeth 2* is indeed a city at sea, equipped for emergencies with a full hospital and operating room, physiotherapy room, and dental surgery facilities. *QE2* has two sets of fin stabilizers which act somewhat like underwater airplane wings, using flaps which reduce the amount of rolling motion. The *QE2* has the use of two sets of bow thrusters to aid her in maneuvering and docking. Twenty-two elevators move passengers and crew, and if desired, up to 80 cars can be carried on the ship. Safety features incorporated for the *QE2*'s passengers include a fire sprinkler system throughout the ship, use of nonflammable materials, a satellite navigation system, and 20 fully-motorized lifeboats.

The final commercial voyage of *QE2*'s

namesake, the *Queen Elizabeth,* was completed on November 5, 1968. The ship had been sold for £3.25 million, and following a farewell visit by Queen Elizabeth, the Queen Mother, the ship departed Southampton on November 29 with a skeleton crew, bound for Port Everglades, Florida. There, she was to be open for tours, similar to the *Queen Mary*'s operation in California, but problems with conversion work, a lack of co-operation with the city officials, and a series of arson fires eventually doomed the project.

The *Queen Elizabeth* was resold in September 1970 to Orient Overseas Line for $3.2 million to become a floating university, sailing around the world with students and a limited number of passengers. She was renamed *Seawise University,* a play on the initials of Orient Overseas's owner, C.Y. Tung. After two years of inactivity in Florida, six of the ship's 12 boilers were brought back to life and the ship made seaworthy to make the voyage

to Hong Kong for conversion.

The former *Queen Elizabeth* departed Florida on February 10, 1971, only to have her boilers fail five days later. She was taken under tow to Aruba, and finally got underway again on May 8 after the renewal of 294 boiler tubes.

A gala welcome greeted her arrival in Hong Kong on July 16, 1971, followed by a $5 million conversion carried out by 1,200 workers. *Seawise University's* maiden voyage was scheduled to begin in Los Angeles in April 1972, but she would never arrive.

The ship was anchored in Hong Kong harbor on January 9, just one week before she was to depart for sea trials and drydocking in Japan. Exterior painting was being completed, and the two huge funnels were already sporting the Orient Overseas Line logo. That afternoon, preparations were being made for a cocktail party in the former First Class Lounge on Promenade Deck. Approximately 60 visitors and over 500 workmen and crew were on board, when at least three fires broke out almost simultaneously. Amazingly, there were no serious injuries as the ship was evacuated.

The fires rapidly merged into one raging inferno, encompassing the entire upper decks. Fireboats and fire trucks mounted on barges quickly came to the scene, but in a scenario reminiscent of the destruction of the *Normandie,* water was ceaselessly pumped onto the upper decks of *Seawise University* until, on the morning of January 10, she slowly turned onto her starboard side, partially sinking into the mud at the bottom of the harbor. The areas where the bridge and elegant Verandah Grill had been located vanished as decks collapsed in the intense heat. The once proud *Queen Elizabeth* was being cut up for scrap as a marine court of inquiry ruled that the probable cause was arson.

TOP LEFT: Construction of the Q4 (eventually named QE2) used prefabricated hull sections, unlike the other Queen liners. RIGHT, TOP TO BOTTOM: Workers labor to install wood paneling in the QE2's passageways, while another inspects the gearbox of one of her auxiliary turbo-generators. Occasionally, there is time for a break. Workers are seen relaxing in the shadow of the nearly-completed ship.

TOP LEFT: Workers oversee progress of QE2 construction. As the QE2 neared her launching date, two 30-ton propellers (TOP RIGHT) were fitted into position, and 1,400 tons of drag chains (BOTTOM RIGHT) were carefully checked to make sure they would stop the ship during the launch. BOTTOM LEFT: the QE2's bulbous bow was another technical innovation over the prior Queen liners.

COMPLETION OF QUEEN ELIZABETH 2

The tides of the Clyde River were carefully calculated in anticipation of the QE2's journey to the sea. His Royal Highness Prince Charles was invited to be the ship's first "passenger" for the trip. The QE2's top officers had been selected months earlier, to oversee the progress of construction. The former captain of the Queen Mary and Queen Elizabeth, William Warwick, was appointed as her first master, along with Chief Officer Robert Arnott and Chief Engineer Jack Marland.

On November 19, 1968, as the time of departure approached, Prince Charles took his place with Captain Warwick on the bridge. Ship traffic came to a halt on the Clyde, and thousands of people assembled to watch the new liner make her way down the river. Her first destination was the King George V drydock at Greenock, Scotland. There she was brought out of the water, for the first time in a year, to have her underwater surfaces scraped and repainted in preparation for her sea trials.

TRIALS AND TRIBULATIONS

John Brown Shipyard (now part of Upper Clyde Shipbuilders) announced with pride that the official gross registered tonnage for the *Queen Elizabeth 2* measured 65,863 tons. This would place her as the fifth largest passenger liner ever built, behind the two *Queens*, the *Normandie*, and the *France*. Gross tonnage does not represent the weight of a ship, but rather the total internal cubic capacity. The actual weight of a ship is expressed in displacement tonnage, but is seldom used when referring to merchant ships. *QE2*'s original displacement tonnage when fully loaded measured 48,886 "long" tons.

John Brown's had planned the *Queen Elizabeth 2*'s acceptance trials for December 4, 1968, but during a series of technical tests, a faulty valve allowed oil to leak into the engines' feed water system. When the handpicked Cunard crew arrived in Scotland, they found the *QE2*'s stateroom and crew areas still unfinished. Frenzied workers toiled simultaneously in both engine and passenger spaces. The 48-hour series of technical tests were again conducted on December 17-18, with the ship steaming the measured mile at a speed of 31.87 knots.

The *Queen Elizabeth 2* departed on a shakedown cruise to the Canary Islands on December 23. On board were 500 passengers, mostly Cunard Line employees and families, plus 200 Clydebank workers, frantically completing the staterooms in time for 75 press representatives, who would embark in Las Palmas. It turned out that the greatest problems were below the passenger decks. On December 26, blades in the *QE2*'s steam turbines failed. Cunard chairman Sir Basil Smallpeice announced that even without the turbine problems, the ship would not have been accepted from the shipyard because of the amount of unfinished work in the passenger areas. The planned January 10 maiden voyage was indefinitely postponed.

The *QE2* limped back to Southampton at 14 knots, to be met by 1,400 workers, who were to repair the turbine damage and complete the interior fittings. The damaged turbines were flown back to Clydebank, and following an independent assessment by Sir Arnold Lindley, president of the Institution of Mechanical Engineers, the malfunction was diagnosed as a design error which caused excessive vibration to the turbine blading.

A second shake-down cruise to Dakar, Senegal, was the final opportunity for the *Queen Elizabeth 2*'s officers and crew to familiarize themselves with the ship's layout and operations. The cruise was completed without incident, and Cunard formally accepted the *QE2* on April 18, 1969. Cunard Line's cost for the *Queen Elizabeth 2* was finally agreed at £29,091,000.

An eight-day cruise, from Southampton to the Canary Islands, departed on April 22 with 1,350 passengers, marking the first commercial voyage for the *QE2*. The ship arrived back in Southampton on April 30, 1969, at last ready for her maiden transatlantic voyage.

The QE2 early in her career.

Chapter Three

The Greatest Ship in the World

The departure of the *Queen Elizabeth 2* from Southampton on May 2, 1969, attracted thousands of people who lined the piers and waterfront as Captain Warwick ordered the *QE2* seaward at 12:45 pm—15 minutes late because of the difficulty in removing the thousands of visitors on board the ship.

The liner's first stop was in Le Havre, France, before she headed west, and by midnight, May 3, *QE2* was 508 miles west of Bishop's Rock. Cunard officials denied any attempt at breaking the *United States*'s 35.5-knot transatlantic speed record; the *QE2* had not been built with that in mind. She steamed past Ambrose Light Tower on May 7, completing the crossing in 4 days, 16 hours, and 35 minutes, averaging a respectable 28.02 knots. The ship's logbook showed that she regularly steamed a comfortable 32 knots during the passage.

The *QE2* passed underneath New York's Verrazano Bridge at 1 pm, escorted by a Coast Guard cutter, helicopters, a pair of British RAF Harrier jets, harbor tugboats and fireboats, a United States Navy destroyer escort, and 150 other small boats. Captain Warwick rang up "Finished With Engines" at 3:12 pm, upon arrival at her New York home at Pier 92.

Mayor John Lindsay proclaimed Queen Elizabeth 2 Day, and that evening, the ship hosted over 2,000 invited guests for dinner and entertainment. The guest list included hundreds of New York socialites, as well as Prince Philip's uncle, Lord Louis Mountbatten, who presented to the Officer's Wardroom an autographed photo-

graph, as he had done on board the *Queen Mary* and *Queen Elizabeth*. Mountbatten sailed on the *QE2*'s maiden eastbound crossing also, along with 1,500 other passengers.

All during her first series of crossings, Cunard worked to identify ways to improve its new ship. For example, some passengers requested a separate towel bar for the bath mat. Convenience for other passengers meant ease in scheduling a round-trip sea voyage. Because the *Queen Elizabeth 2* and the French Line's *France* were the only liners left on the Atlantic in late 1969, the two lines arranged to share pier facilities in New York, and planned alternate weekly sailing schedules.

Between her maiden voyage and the end of September 1969, the *Queen Elizabeth 2* completed 11 transatlantic round-trip voyages, during which the ship made a profit of £1,674,000. The design and operations of the *Queen Elizabeth 2* were a great success.

An interesting series of sea trials were held for the *QE2* on April 5, 1970, between Lisbon and Le Havre. The British Board of Trade requested that a "crash test" be made to determine the ability of the ship to stop and reverse under emergency circumstances. The remarkable power of the *Queen Elizabeth 2*'s engines was demonstrated, as the ship was slowed from 29.5 knots to 8.5 knots only four minutes after the full astern order was given. Two and a half minutes later, the *QE2* was dead in the water, and within eight and a half minutes from the initial order, she was travelling astern at four and a half knots.

TOP: The Queen Elizabeth 2 is welcomed in typical New York style as she reaches her destination. BOTTOM: The QE2 departs Southampton on her maiden voyage, May 2, 1969.

RESCUE ON THE HIGH SEAS

On the afternoon of January 8, 1971, passengers on board the 20,419-ton French Line cruise ship *Antilles* were steaming past the Leeward Islands, 450 miles southeast of Puerto Rico, enjoying the first full day of a relaxing nine-day Caribbean cruise. Suddenly their ship struck an offshore reef, tearing open fuel tanks in the bottom of the ship, as the *Antilles* literally ground to a halt on the sharp coral. The fuel quickly ignited, and though the flames were fought bravely by the ship's crew, Captain Raymond Kerverdo gave the order to abandon ship an hour after the collision.

Most passengers on board the *Antilles* thought that boarding the lifeboats was merely a precaution. They did not know of the frantic fire-fighting efforts being made far below them. Fortunately, this atmosphere led to the very calm evacuation of 648 passengers and 340 crew members. Even as the survivors made their way to shore, explosions were rocking the *Antilles,* spreading the fire throughout the ship.

At 7:05 pm, an SOS signal was received by the *Queen Elizabeth 2* from the *Antilles,* reading "Aground and afire." When the *Queen Elizabeth 2* arrived on the scene at 10:30 pm, she found a chilling sight. The eerie glow of the fires aboard the *Antilles* lit the area, which was scattered with empty life rafts floating nearby. One QE2 passenger said, "You could almost feel the heat. We were terrified that there were people still on the ship."

By radio, it was discovered with relief that everyone on board the *Antilles* had been removed safely. The job of transporting 501 of the passengers from the island of Mustique to the *Queen Elizabeth 2* lasted almost four hours because of heavy seas and strong winds. Amazingly, there were no injuries throughout the entire operation.

STORM AT SEA

Storms on the North Atlantic are legendary, but the one which hit the *QE2* in April 1972 was one which almost defied description. The *Queen Elizabeth 2* was one day out of New York when she entered the 1,500-mile-wide storm termed "worse than a hurricane" by Captain Mortimer Hehir. It embroiled the ship in 100-mile-per-hour winds and 50-foot-high seas for three days. About $6,000 worth of glassware and china were smashed, along with eight of the huge Upper Deck windows and two pianos which had come loose from their moorings when the ship rolled at an angle of up to 22 degrees. Forced to slow to 5 knots by the intensity of the storm, the *QE2* arrived in Southampton 36 hours late.

Despite the success of the *Queen Elizabeth 2,* overall passenger ship traffic was suffering in 1970. Following two years of profits for Cunard, the company was ripe for a take-over bid. Shortly after an unusual price increase in Cunard stock on June 29, 1971, an offer of £2.10 a share was made by Trafalgar House Investments, a diverse British property and construction corporation. The final board meeting on August 25, 1971, was the end of Cunard as an independent company, but the beginning of a great opportunity to combine the shipping operations with Trafalgar House's hotel and leisure properties.

The annual overhaul of the *QE2* in Fall 1972 included several major modifications. The capacity of the Britannia and Columbia Restaurants was increased by 256 to accommodate all passengers at one sitting, allowing the *QE2* a one class operation while cruising. The former 736 Club on Boat Deck was transformed into the now famous Queen's Grill, and enlarged to seat 196 passengers. The Queen's Grill Lounge was created, using the space formerly occupied by The Coffee Shop and teenagers' club, The Juke Box. New kitchens were installed to service the Queen's Grill, while the other restaurants' kitchens were expanded on Upper Deck, forward of the Britannia Restaurant, eliminating The Look-Out Bar. The Cunard-Marlborough London Gallery, a unique feature of the *QE2* showing selected original fine art, was replaced by a quiet reading room, decorated with paintings and photographs of famous Cunard ships. Three new bars were created, while the shops on Boat Deck were moved aft to the upper level of the Double Room.

TOP: The QE2 in 1969.
ABOVE: The Queen's Room in the late Sixties.

The Casino Bar (TOP LEFT) is a place for a momentary rest from the excitement of the QE2's Players Club Casino. TOP RIGHT: The Queen's Grill is famous for its fine dining and service. Expanded kitchen facilities took the place of the old Look-out Bar (ABOVE MIDDLE) in 1972.

DANGER IN THE MIDDLE EAST

The year 1973 brought one of the *Queen Elizabeth 2*'s most hazardous passenger cruises. A Massachusetts travel agency chartered the ship for a cruise to Israel to celebrate the country's 25th anniversary. Security measures not seen in Southampton since World War II were in effect to guard against any type of terrorist attack. The number of persons guarding the gangways was tripled, and Royal Navy frogmen regularly searched for mines under the *QE2*'s hull. Normal x-ray and searching procedures were in operation, and no visitors or spectators were allowed near the ship.

From the moment passengers landed in England aboard six chartered jets, they were provided with a huge police escort. Thirty special guards, including some posing as passengers, sailed with the 620 passengers and 900 crew members. Security was not the only special preparation that had to be made for the cruise. The entire Columbia Restaurant kitchen was made kosher for the cruise, and 11 rabbis made sure that Jewish dietary laws were observed.

The *Queen Elizabeth 2* departed Southampton on April 16, 1973, bound for Lisbon, Portugal. She immediately changed her normal course to one which took her far from the North African coast. Precautions didn't diminish, as Lisbon's Salazar suspension bridge over the Tagus River was closed as the *QE2* passed underneath and 23 Portuguese frogmen made regular searches of the ship's hull during the 12 hours *QE2* was at her berth.

As she entered Israeli waters, the normally bright lights aboard the *Queen Elizabeth 2* were blacked out. British military ships and planes were rumored to have shadowed the liner throughout the cruise. The *QE2* berthed in Ashdod, Israel, for four days, then steamed on to Haifa. On April 29, the cruise was reversed, and the ship arrived safely back in Southampton on May 13.

Despite all the security arrangements, Staff Captain Douglas Ridley described his part of the cruise as "monotonous," and stated that "The only threats I know of are what we have read in the newspapers." Ridley did not know until a year later that their lives had been in danger during the cruise. On July 16, 1974, Egyptian President Anwar Sadat told BBC television that he had personally countermanded an order given

by another Arab leader to torpedo the *QE2* during the Israel cruise. He was later identified as Libya's Colonel Moammar Khadafy.

In April 1974, more difficulty struck the *Queen Elizabeth 2,* as she suffered a boiler malfunction while on a Caribbean cruise. The liner was 280 miles southwest of Bermuda when an alarm signaled the presence of an impurity in the boiler feed water. The engines were automatically shut down, but not in time to prevent contaminating fuel oil from spreading through the system.

Two tugboats were sent to tow the *QE2* to Bermuda in case repairs could not be made at sea. Emergency generators kept the ship's lights on, but the air conditioning and refrigeration systems could not be used. Cunard decided to remove the *QE2*'s passengers to Flagship Cruises' ship *Sea Venture,* better known later as the *Pacific Princess*.

The 20,000-ton *Sea Venture* arrived on April 3, with 202 passengers of her own, ready to take aboard 1,648 more from the *Queen Elizabeth 2.* The transfer operation lasted seven hours, and was accomplished without mishap to any of the passengers. The *Sea Venture* made her way back to Bermuda, where the *QE2*'s passengers were flown back to New York.

Thanks to the ability of the Cunard staff, the majority of the passengers took the whole affair as a great adventure. One 70-year-old passenger summed up her adventure by saying, "I won't take another cruise until they have one like this."

On January 10, 1975, the *Queen Elizabeth 2* was ready to embark on her Premier World Cruise. She called at 22 different ports on four continents, including exotic cities such as Rio de Janeiro, Cape Town, Bombay, Singapore, Bali, Hong Kong, and Acapulco. The "long cruise" was to become a yearly tradition.

Trouble again struck the ship on July 23, 1976, when a fire broke out in the *Queen Elizabeth 2*'s engine room. The ship was steaming about 80 miles off the Scilly Islands southwest of England, headed toward New York, when an electrical malfunction set fire to lubricating oil, and burned for 50 minutes before it could be brought under control. A 20-year-old engineer, Kenneth Lyon, was seriously burned. The *Queen Elizabeth 2* limped back to Southampton sporting a blackened funnel.

LEFT: The QE2 arrives in Newport News, Virginia, for repairs to her bow, after hitting submerged coral in January 1976. RIGHT: Passengers wave to the QE2 after being transferred to the Sea Venture following a boiler malfunction in the Caribbean.

FACELIFT FOR A QUEEN

The *Queen Elizabeth 2* is overhauled annually at Southampton, when every inch of the ship is checked over, cleaned, renewed, or replaced. This includes everything from inspection of the engine machinery and renovation of the public rooms and passenger staterooms, to the addition of any new features which may be felt required. The ship is put into drydock to have the outside of the hull scraped of marine growth and a new coat of paint applied.

Special repairs needed in January 1977 required part of the work to be moved to Bayonne, New Jersey, where the *QE2* was in drydock for 10 days. A new set of turbine blades replaced the ones damaged in the engine room fire, and permanent repairs were made to the bulbous bow following the ship's having struck a coral reef a year earlier.

Economically, having the repairs done in the United States made sense for Cunard, so much that the *QE2* returned to New Jersey for her full overhaul at the end of both 1977 and 1979. It was in 1977 that the Queen Mary and Queen Elizabeth suites, designed by Dennis Lennon, were added onto the *QE2*'s Signal Deck. Each prefabricated suite, weighing 15 tons and measuring 50 by 30 feet, was lifted into place forward of the Trafalgar and Queen Anne Suites.

At the same time, the Britannia Restaurant became more international in flavor, adopting English, French, Spanish, Italian, and Oriental themes. As the new Tables of the World restaurant, the room was capable of seating 882 passengers.

The QE2's 1977 overhaul included the installation of prefabricated Queen Mary and Queen Elizabeth suites, and conversion of the Britannia Restaurant to the multi-nationally themed Tables of the World.

QE2: Cruising the World

A grand tradition for the *Queen Elizabeth 2* began on January 10, 1975, as she departed New York on what was billed her Premier World Cruise, an 80-day around-the-world voyage, emulating the journey of Jules Verne's character Phineas Fogg. A history-making voyage it was too! The *QE2* became the largest vessel to pass through the Panama Canal, and her passengers were the first large group to travel through the People's Republic of China since World War II. In all, 3,965 passengers took part in the historic 37,963-mile voyage.

The Great Pacific and Orient Cruise of 1978 was the *QE2*'s first "circle cruise." Instead of travelling completely around the world, the ship left New York, travelled through the Panama Canal to Acapulco and Los Angeles, then across the Pacific making first-time visits to harbors in Tahiti, Tonga, Fiji, New Zealand, Australia, New Guinea, and San Francisco. Each time she passes through the Panama Canal, the *Queen Elizabeth 2* pays the largest toll of any other ship: $82,000. Returning to New York 90 days later, she had steamed over 39,000 miles to 31 different ports.

The 1980 World Cruise was the *QE2*'s Tenth Anniversary Celebration, and the highlight was her maiden transit of the Suez Canal. Having passed through the Panama Canal earlier in the cruise, the *QE2* became the largest vessel to transit both canals on the same voyage. This trip also marked her famous maiden call to Yalta, in the Soviet Union.

In 1985, the *Queen Elizabeth 2* explored the "Golden Route:" 95 days around the world. For passengers only taking a portion of the cruise, British Airways' Concorde was used for the first time to speed them to the *QE2* upon arrival in Sydney, Hong Kong, Singapore, Cape Town, and Rio de Janeiro. Passengers on the January 1986 cruise were urged to "Capture the Spirit of the Explorers" as the *QE2* made seven maiden arrivals in a total of 33 ports. For the first time, the ship travelled to Cancun, Mexico; Puerto Limon, Costa Rica; Lima, Peru; Valparaiso and Puerto Montt in Chile; and around the tip of South America through the Straits of Magellan. Following her Far East leg of the voyage, she returned to New York via the Panama Canal. This was to be her last extended cruise before her 1986-87 refit.

The "new" *QE2* travelled "The Voyage of the Southern Crown" in 1988, taking her through the Panama Canal to familiar ports in Acapulco, Los Angeles, Tahiti, New Zealand, Australia, Bombay, Singapore, Bangkok, and Hong Kong, prior to two new ports, Shanghai and Beijing, China. Her passengers were given a special view of a total solar eclipse before returning through the Panama Canal to New York 107 days later.

The *Queen Elizabeth 2*'s January cruise has proven to be extremely popular, and takes her to new and exotic portions of the world each year.

The QE2's departure from Southampton (UPPER RIGHT) takes her out past "The Needles" and the white cliffs of Dover at the mouth of the Solent River. Each port on the ship's "long cruise" provides her with a gala reception, such as in Sydney, Australia (BOTTOM LEFT). The QE2 visits many exotic ports of call on her world cruise (BOTTOM RIGHT).

STORMY WEATHER

In late September 1978, the *Queen Elizabeth 2* survived one of the worst North Atlantic storms of her career. Force 12 winds (the maximum on the Beaufort scale) were recorded up to 70 mph, and along with 50-foot waves, they slowed the ship's speed to nine knots. Hundreds of pieces of china were broken and waves twisted the iron railings surrounding the bow, occasionally reaching as high as the *QE2*'s bridge.

1979 celebrated the *QE2*'s 10th year in service, marked by a world cruise with the theme, "For Once in Your Life, Live!" She called at 24 ports in 14 countries, but upon her return to New York on April 8, she was greeted by a tugboat strike. Captains of the *Queen Mary* and *Queen Elizabeth* had docked without tugs before, but they did not have the advantage of the *QE2*'s bow thruster propellers.

Captain Douglas Ridley had to take into account the wind conditions, strong tidal flow of the Hudson River, and the narrow 400-foot opening between the two piers into which he had to turn his 105-foot wide ship. Slowing the *QE2* down to six knots, Captain Ridley slightly misjudged the strength of the underwater current, and as the bow was nearing the far pier, he quickly reversed the *QE2* back out into the river. His second attempt was successful, and 1,050 relieved passengers were able to depart the ship.

The world oil crisis in 1979 severely affected not only the price of gasoline, but also the cost of bunker "C" fuel oil, which the *Queen Elizabeth 2* consumes at the rate of 300 tons per day while cruising and a staggering 500 tons per day on Atlantic crossings. The cost of fuel for the ship that year jumped to an alarming $20 million. Along with rising crew wages, this forced Cunard Line to announce the possible withdrawal of the ship in 1980. Fortunately, cost-saving measures allowed the firm to avoid this gloomy prospect.

INTERNATIONAL INTRIGUE

Occasionally the *Queen Elizabeth 2* becomes involved in international politics. One of her first encounters was during her 1980 World Cruise, when she made her first call in the Crimean resort city of Yalta. Tension was high between the United States and the Soviet Union, with the American boycott of the 1980 Olympics in Moscow. When the *QE2* dropped her anchor, Soviet immigration officials boarded the ship, but as time went by, they became more difficult, insisting on checking every passenger's passport, and then demanding that each person have a full Soviet entry visa or prepaid tour ticket. This eliminated approximately half of the *QE2*'s passengers from going ashore.

Captain Robert Arnott sensed the growing anxiety of his passengers, and met with the head Soviet immigration official. Just as the first passenger launch from the *QE2* was about to reach the pier, Captain Arnott ordered it back to the ship. He would not allow the Soviets to grant certain passengers immediate permission to go ashore, others to suffer long delays, and many not to be able to go ashore at all.

Despite the hardship, the *QE2*'s passengers strongly supported Captain Arnott's decision. One passenger wrote later about the incident to the New York *Times* saying, "Captain Arnott's gutsy decision was overwhelmingly applauded by the passengers. One can only guess the impact of his reaction on the Russians ashore, who had made elaborate preparations for the visit by 1,500 passengers plus crew." Being the captain of a liner like the *Queen Elizabeth 2* may be a glamorous job at times, but certainly only the finest of Cunard's officers can be chosen for this important position.

THE QUEEN GOES TO WAR

A military action over a small group of frigid islands in the Southern Atlantic was to have a dramatic influence on the history of Great Britain, Argentina, and the *Queen Elizabeth 2*. As 1982 began, Argentina began to threaten invasion of the Atlantic Falkland Islands. The Falklands, named the Malvinas by nearby Argentina, were first settled by the British in 1766, and had remained a source of contention ever since. At dawn on April 2, an Argentine invasion fleet unexpectedly attacked Port Stanley, the small capital of the Falkland Islands. The city was defended by only 80 Royal Marines, who were quickly subdued. The British were outraged, and three days later sent a task force of over 100 ships to reclaim the islands. The battle escalated quickly into a full-scale war.

During the early stages of the conflict, the *Queen Elizabeth 2* was keeping to her scheduled transatlantic crossings, but as actions in the South Atlantic escalated, rumors began of British vessels being requisitioned to carry British troops to the remote islands. The P&O liner *Canberra* had already departed Southampton on April 9 with three battalions of soldiers.

On May 3, the British BBC news announced

that the *QE2* would be requisitioned as a troopship. Upon her arrival in Southampton, Cunard's Captain Peter Jackson took command of the ship as preparations were made to outfit the ship to carry 3,000 soldiers.

A huge steel helicopter landing area was fitted over the *QE2*'s forward docking equipment, while the outdoor swimming pools at the stern were covered over to make two more landing pads. Thousands of square feet of plywood were placed together to protect the ship's bulkheads and carpeting, while areas such as the Double Room were converted into mess halls. Sophisticated navy navigational aids were added to the *QE2*'s own satellite navigation and radar systems. Removed from the ship were valuable pieces of art and furniture, as well as her china and silverware.

The first members of the 5th Infantry Brigade began to board the *Queen Elizabeth 2* on May 12, including 2nd Battalion The Scots Guards, 1st Battalion The Welsh Guards, and 1st Battalion of the famous 7th Duke of Edinburgh's Own Gurkha Rifles from Nepal. Seven hundred of *Queen Elizabeth 2*'s regular crew volunteered to stay with the ship. Also aboard was 37-year-old artist Linda Kitson, commissioned by the Imperial War Museum to sketch the troops as they participated in the battle. Supplies and ammunition arrived to equip the ship for a three-month voyage, including 9,000 paperback books, 3 million Mars candy bars, and 432,000 cans of beer!

Relatives and friends gathered with thousands of other well-wishers to bid the ship farewell that day, but the *Queen Elizabeth 2* almost missed her 4 pm sailing schedule. Two of her three boilers developed massive leaks in their feed water systems. In spite of these problems, the partially-disabled ship did depart, to the echo of sirens, car horns, and whistles down the entire length of the Solent River. She was now a member of STUFT, a typical military acronym for "Ships Taken Up From Trade."

Once out of sight of land, the *QE2* dropped anchor to resolve her boiler troubles. An overnight trouble-shooting search found the problem to be simply a valve which had been left open. The ship finally got underway for the South Atlantic at 9:30 the next morning.

Daily routines quickly settled in. Specific times for each company were laid out for activities such as boat drills, jogging around the decks in full packs, and small arms practice. The Gurkhas, known for their tight discipline, became proficient at finding their lifeboat stations blindfolded.

Five days after departing Southampton, the *Queen Elizabeth 2* entered the African harbor of Freetown, berthing at a pier specially secured with walls of stacked cargo containers. There, she took on fuel and fresh water, and was underway again in 11 hours. Other vessels on their way to the Falklands kept in close contact, often transferring supplies by helicopter. The helicopters were also used to receive supplies from *HMS Dumbarton Castle* and the base at Ascension Island.

Just prior to passing Ascension Island on May 21, news was received that British troops had landed at San Carlos on East Falkland. This led to the successful reclaiming of the islands, but much battle still lay ahead. Preparations for war began in earnest, using some of the various types of defensive weapons which had been installed on the ship, including anti-aircraft missiles at the base of the funnel and Browning machine guns on each bridge wing.

The *Queen Elizabeth 2* ran into colder weather as she proceeded on her southerly course, but the news received on May 25 was as gloomy as the weather. Word came that the Argentines had sunk *HMS Coventry,* sister ship to the *HMS Sheffield* lost on May 4, and also the Cunard container ship *Atlantic Conveyor.* Twenty VTOL Harrier aircraft had departed the Cunarder, flying to the aircraft carrier *HMS Hermes,* shortly before the *Conveyor* was hit by two Exocet missiles. Its loss forced the crew aboard *QE2* to realize the danger that they faced on their mission.

The Argentines were not the only hazard as the *Queen Elizabeth 2* entered a heavy iceberg zone in low visibility. Use of the *QE2*'s radar had to be avoided because of the ability of modern weapons systems to home in on its signal. However, on May 26, the situation became so critical that the ship's speed was reduced to 9 knots, and the radar switched on every half hour to reveal the presence of at least 100 icebergs in the surrounding area. One was estimated to be a mile long and 300 feet high. The murky conditions, which could be so dangerous, kept the *QE2* hidden from Argentine aircraft in a veil of fog and mist. A defensive zig-zag course was begun once the ship was clear of the iceberg field.

A helicopter lands on one of the QE2's after landing pads. Practice landings were commonplace in preparation for arrival in the Falkland Islands.

On May 27, the *Queen Elizabeth 2* reached her destination: South Georgia. She anchored in Cumberland Bay, having steamed 8,000 miles from Southampton. The small harbor was approximately a mile away from Grytviken, the whaling village where a group of Argentines originally had raised their flag, touching off the original hostilities.

Calm seas and foggy weather continued, and by midnight, the QE2's "passengers" began to disembark onto four large trawlers. The troops were then transferred to the P&O ferry *Norland* and the liner *Canberra,* which had unloaded her soldiers right at the battlefront. Both would deliver QE2's troops to the beachhead at San Carlos Bay. In return, QE2 boarded 374 survivors from the sinkings of *HMS Ardent* and *HMS Antelope.* The QE2 remained anchored as her supplies were unloaded. Some of these supplies, along with 400 additional troops, went aboard the *HMS Stromness,* in return for 255 survivors from the sinking of *HMS Coventry.*

On the afternoon of May 29, rough weather and reports of a nearby Argentine air attack led the *Queen Elizabeth 2* to leave South Georgia and head back to sea. By the time the ship was secured and had raised anchor, the wind had risen to full gale strength. The weather postponed transfer of fuel from the tanker *Bayleaf* for two days, but down to less than 1,000 tons of fuel, the QE2 was forced to take on additional fuel despite the heavy seas. The hazardous but vital process took over nine and a half hours and supplied the QE2 with almost 4,000 tons of fuel.

On June 5, the ship neared Ascension Island, and it was guessed that the 629 survivors would disembark there, so the *Queen Elizabeth 2* could return to the Falklands, possibly with an additional load of fresh troops. The Cunard crew had mixed opinions, as many were prepared to stay at sea longer, pointing to the brave work being done by P&O's liner *Canberra.* However, with the war in the Falklands now favoring the British, the QE2 was ordered to head home for Southampton to personally deliver her war heros. Supplies were again delivered from *HMS Dumbarton Castle* by helicopter, and removed ammunition and material which had not been able to be unloaded in South Georgia.

The *Queen Elizabeth 2*'s welcome to Southampton on June 11 began with a visit by the commander in chief of the Royal Navy, Admiral John Fieldhouse, who landed on board to speak to the survivors and crew. The highlight of the welcome was the personal greeting by Her Majesty Queen Elizabeth, the Queen Mother, who waved to the soldiers from the after deck of the Royal Yacht *Britannia.* Thousands of people lined the shores of the Solent River, joined by helicopters, light aircraft, and hundreds of boats escorting the *Queen Elizabeth 2* to her berth.

Even as the welcome grew, anticipation of reunions with family members was first on the minds and hearts of both the survivors and crew members. Occasionally, a scream of recognition was heard as the QE2 passed by her berth at the Queen Elizabeth II terminal in order to turn around and dock on her port side. By noon, the first gangway was down and relatives of the injured were allowed on board.

During her troop service, the *Queen Elizabeth 2* had steamed 14,967 miles through rough seas, near zero visibility, icebergs, under threat of missile and torpedo attack, had experienced helicopter landings and take-offs, been refueled at sea, and successfully transported 3,000 soldiers to battle and 629 heroic veterans home again. She had indeed proven herself as a proud Cunarder at war.

Upon arrival in South Georgia, the soldiers aboard the QE2 *disembarked onto large trawlers, adapted for the duty, and readied for onshore battle.*

RETURN TO PEACETIME

The use of the *Queen Elizabeth 2* in the Falkland Islands war gave Cunard Line the unique opportunity to make major modifications to the ship while the implements of war were being removed. Work began on June 12, 1982, the day following her triumphant entry into Southampton. She was put into drydock to have regular maintenance work done on her underwater areas, and to allow easy access for removal of the huge helicopter landing pads.

Cunard took this occasion to speed up the first phase of the refurbishment of the Q4 Room on Quarter Deck. This room became the Club Lido, with new sliding glass doors to the Quarter Deck Pool. This pool would be fitted with the retractable Magrodome in 1983. The indoor Six Deck pool was refurbished with a travelling version of the famous Golden Door Spa in Southern California. The program had begun as a temporary amenity during the 1982 World Cruise. The Golden Door offers personalized aerobic, diet, and water exercise programs plus three new Jacuzzi whirlpool baths.

The Queens Grill Restaurant was redesigned by Dennis Lennon, using new cobalt blue and green colors with silver trim. The Queens Grill Lounge was also redecorated, adding an intimate bar. The *QE2*'s casino was renamed the Player's Club and enlarged, incorporating a new color scheme and new adjoining lounge. The ship's air conditioning and heating systems were substantially increased for passengers' comfort on cruises and the cold North Atlantic. Artwork, furniture, and china, removed prior to the conflict, were brought out of storage and returned to their proper locations.

On the outside, the *QE2* boasted of new colors—a light pebble-grey hull with traditional red and black Cunard Line funnel colors. Upon seeing the new grey hull color, most people assumed that it had been adopted as camouflage for the Falklands, but it was a post-war addition. Altogether, the British Government spent $3.4 million for repairs and conversion of the *Queen Elizabeth 2,* while Cunard spent an additional $8.4 million. While it had taken only seven days to outfit the ship for war, refurbishing the *QE2* for peacetime service required almost nine weeks.

The end of 1983 was a busy period for the *QE2* and her crew. During her normally hurried turnaround in New York, she played hostess to a special party celebrating the 60th anniversary of *Time* magazine. On October 23, five members of the crew joined 17,000 other runners in the famous New York City Marathon. In order to start the race on time, the crew members had to be taken off the *QE2* by launch as she passed under the Verrazano Bridge. Despite the obstacles, all five finished the race.

On November 28, the *Queen Elizabeth 2* arrived in Bremerhaven, Germany, for her annual overhaul, which included the installation of the new retractable, all-weather Magrodome over the Quarter Deck Pool.

The highlight of 1986 was the *QE2*'s participation in the 100th anniversary of the dedication of the Statue of Liberty on July 4. New York Harbor was the scene for what must have been one of the biggest celebrations in history. The *Queen Elizabeth 2* was indeed the jewel out of the thousands of boats, naval vessels, and tall ships anchored in the harbor for the festivities. The Cunard Line was proud of the *QE2*, and what they had planned for the end of 1986 would ensure that their ship would remain Queen of the Seas.

TOP: The QE2 took part in the centennial of the Statue of Liberty. BOTTOM: The Queen Elizabeth 2 arrives in New York following her 1987 refit.

Chapter Four

Superliner for the 21st Century

In 1986, the *Queen Elizabeth 2* celebrated her 17th year in service. While the first *Queen Elizabeth* had steamed through 29 years, and the *Queen Mary* 31 years, one of the main factors for the end of their careers at sea resulted from the astronomical increase in the price of fuel oil. Steam turbine engines like those on board the *QE2* burn hundreds of tons of fuel every day. The Cunard Line knew that in order to keep the *QE2* financially afloat through the end of the 20th century, major modifications were needed. Experts said from the day of her launch that another liner like the *Queen Elizabeth 2* would never again be built, but estimates to replace her were upwards of $400 million.

The problem, and the solution, was in her engines. The same type of engines which had powered the *Mauretania* and *Lusitania* almost 80 years earlier was too inefficient for today's superliner. The decision was made to take the *Queen Elizabeth 2* out of service for six months to be completely re-engined and refurbished. The *QE2* originally cost $70.8 million to construct, and an estimated $30 million had been spent by Cunard on additional improvements between 1982 and 1986. A further $130 million would be spent during the 179-day re-fit—a costly $726,000 a day! Cunard could have built a medium-sized cruise ship for the same price, but she wouldn't be a queen!

Two and a half years of research was devoted to the choice of engines for the *QE2*. Fuel efficiency, overall operating costs, and reliability were explored, as well as the *QE2*'s unique need for prolonged high speed on the North Atlantic. The company investigated more than 15 engine options between August 1983 and September 1985.

After examining the ability of potential shipyards to schedule and complete the work in a short amount of time, Cunard selected the Lloyd Werft shipyard in Bremerhaven, Germany. Its experience and long history of working with cruise ships, including the transformation of the transatlantic liner *France* into the Caribbean cruise liner *Norway*, was a large factor in their choice. Lloyd Werft was also expert in completing work rapidly and on schedule, two important factors for Cunard. The contract was signed in October 1985 for what would be the largest merchant marine re-fit in history. All shipyard work on the liner had to be completed in 179 days, but design and preparation work had to be ready for the *QE2*'s arrival just one year away. A diesel-electric main propulsion system was chosen for the *Queen Elizabeth 2*, which would give her excellent reliability, flexibility in equipment operation, greater fuel economy at varied operating speeds, and a minimum of vibration and noise. The new system uses nine medium-speed diesel engines connected to AC electric generators, which pro-

vide energy for motors operating the propellers, as well as electrical energy for the rest of the ship. Each generator has an output of 10,625 kilowatts at 400 rpm, supplying 10,000 volts. They are bolted to the deck and joined with a flexible coupling to their engines, which are mounted on angled rubber seatings to avoid vibration. Each of the nine engine/generator assemblies weigh 220 tons.

Despite some loss of economy due to the extra electrical generating step involved, the system's efficiency is achieved by the ability of the diesel engines to constantly work at their most efficient speed. Two GEC propulsion motors turn the propellers at 72 revolutions per minute at speeds less than 18 knots, and at 144 rpm above 18 knots The propulsion motors receive electricity from the generators through synchroconverters, and in turn provide up to 59,864 horsepower (44,000 kilowatts) to each propeller. Exact speed is determined by adjusting the blade angle of the two new variable pitch propellers. Each five-bladed propeller is 19 feet in diameter, and weighs almost 42 tons.

The *Queen Elizabeth 2* made her last transatlantic crossing under steam propulsion reaching Southampton on October 25, 1986. Lloyd Werft was ready for her arrival in Bremerhaven, two days later. Teams immediately went to work in various areas of the ship. The entire exterior of the *QE2* was grit-blasted to remove all old paint, and make her ready for primer and fresh coats both above and below the waterline. The old six-bladed propellers and shafting were removed, and replaced with the controllable pitch propellers.

Work was underway above deck to cut away the *Queen Elizabeth 2*'s distinctive funnel. Once the funnel was lifted clear, the previous smoke hatch allowed access to remove the steam turbine machinery and install the new engines. First the two 350-ton propulsion motors were lowered into the ship onto sliding mechanisms, using hydraulic rams to push them into position. The nine engines and generators were next; five units in the after engine room, and four in the forward engine room.

The old high and low pressure turbine assemblies (BELOW) were removed to make room for the nine MAN B&W diesel engine/ generator assemblies (ABOVE AND RIGHT), forming the QE2's new power plant.

Cunard and the Royal Family

The British Royal Family has always had a special relationship with the Cunard Line and their ships. When, in 1934, Her Majesty Queen Mary christened the ship which bore her name, she became the first reigning Queen of Britain to launch a merchant ship. Her daughter-in-law Queen Elizabeth, now the Queen Mother, continued the tradition in 1938.

The present Royal Family has also shown great interest in the *Queen Elizabeth 2*. As early as July 1967, Prince Philip toured the *QE2,* then under construction in Clydebank, and had lunch with representatives of Cunard and John Brown Shipyard. At the ship's launch, Her Majesty Queen Elizabeth II used the same scissors as her mother and grandmother to cut the cord releasing the bottle of champagne. Prince Charles, then 16 years old, blew the ship's whistle to signal the *QE2'*s departure from the shipyard.

On the eve of the *Queen Elizabeth 2'*s maiden trans-atlantic voyage, Her Majesty Queen Elizabeth II and Prince Philip again visited the ship while in Southampton. The Queen toured almost every area of the ship and viewed the bust of herself in the Queen's Room. The Prince's uncle, Lord Louis Mountbatten, sailed on her eastbound maiden voyage from New York. Prince Philip again visited the *QE2* on May 29, 1969, for a special meeting of the Council of Industrial Design, presenting an award to the designers of the *QE2'*s dining room chairs.

Another tradition was continued as Her Majesty Queen Elizabeth II presented the *QE2'*s Officers' Wardroom with portraits of herself and Prince Philip. The two prior *Queen* liners were given the same honor.

The Queen Mother saluted the *QE2* in June 1982 from aboard the Royal Yacht *Britannia,* as the liner returned from her duty in the Falkland Islands war with survivors of the sinkings of three British naval vessels. A plaque bearing the messages exchanged on that occasion was presented to Cunard Line's Lord Matthews and Captain Peter Jackson during a visit by the Queen Mother in December 1982. It is proudly displayed between the personal standards of Their Majesties Queen Mary and Queen Elizabeth, which sailed with the two liners throughout their Cunard service. Three huge tapestries hang nearby, showing the launch of the *Queen Elizabeth 2* by Her Majesty in September 1967.

The latest visit to the *Queen Elizabeth 2* was by Princess Diana, who toured the *QE2* just prior to her post-refit maiden voyage in April 1987. A suitable plaque marking this occasion also hangs in the ship.

TOP: *Elizabeth, the Queen Mother, then-Princess Elizabeth, and her daughter Princess Margaret inspect the* Queen Elizabeth *with Sir Percy Bates just prior to her maiden passenger voyage. BOTTOM RIGHT: Her Majesty Queen Elizabeth II and her sister, Princess Margaret, wave to the men atop the hull as the* QE2 *is launched into the Clyde River. BOTTOM LEFT: Princess Diana speaks with Captain Lawrence Portet after unveiling a plaque aboard the recently-refitted* QE2.

The new diesel engines required the old funnel to be modified and expanded. Instead of needing only two exhaust vents from the three boilers, nine uptakes had to be squeezed into the enlarged funnel, plus air intakes capable of supplying 18,000,000 cubic feet of air per hour to the new diesels and engine spaces. Space utilization was critical, so the entire engine system was constructed first in a 1/20 scale model.

The nine uptakes carrying the hot exhaust gasses from the diesel engines were fitted with waste heat boilers in order to produce steam for heating, kitchen, and other uses. Up to 74 percent of all waste heat can be utilized. Two auxiliary oil-fired boilers were also installed for periods when the main diesels were not producing enough exhaust heat.

While major work was taking place with the propulsion system at the bottom of the ship, the QE2 also experienced a great deal of change above. On the Signal Deck, eight new suites were built aft of the 1972 suites, now aesthetically completing the row of suites between the mast and funnel. The hallway serving the suites is decorated with a deep blue carpeting and attractive art deco-style lighting fixtures. Platou Ship Design of Oslo, Norway, was challenged to connect the existing corridor with the new suites, enlarge the pantry, while taking into account the greater-than-normal stress and extra flexibility required in this area of the ship.

The Boat Deck features changes both inside and out. The overall look of the ship was greatly enhanced by the replacement of the lifeboat davits, now painted white, to match the superstructure. The ship's most elegant restaurant, the Queen's Grill, was enlarged to accommodate the passengers housed in the new suites. The famous polished wood relief of the Royal coat of arms retains its place as the focal point of the room. Adjacent to the Grill on the starboard side is the Queen's Grill Lounge, which has been redecorated in similar design. The port side previously had housed the Computer Learning Center, and earlier the Reading Room. The Computer Learning Center has been expanded and relocated to the forward end of Two Deck. Replacing it is the Executive Board Room. The long design of the Board Room lends itself to a 30-foot conference table, and with its modular design can be adapted to more private meetings or cocktail parties.

TOP: The QE2's new larger funnel gives her a more distinctive look. The color scheme of the Queen's Grill (BOTTOM LEFT) and adjoining Queen's Grill Lounge (BOTTOM RIGHT) has been lightened, using white chairs with ebony wood trim.

Just aft of the entrance to the theatre balcony and Boat Deck suites is the upper level of the Double Room, renamed the Grand Lounge. The redesigned Shopping Promenade is filled with double the number of new individual shops, featuring luxury names such as Christian Dior, Gucci, Pringle of Scotland, H. Stern, Louis Vuitton, and Alfred Dunhill. The *Queen Elizabeth 2* is the first cruise ship to offer tuxedo rental service at sea, thanks to the new Louis Feraud Shop. The aft end of Boat Deck was extended 50 feet to house five additional shops, which include the British Design Shop, Cruise Wear, and the QE2 Logo Shop. The only seagoing branch of Harrods Department Store, which was established in 1984, is still located on One Deck near the D stairway.

The former Tables of the World on Upper Deck has been renamed the Mauretania Restaurant. The largest restaurant on the *QE2,* it has been beautifully redecorated with numerous rare photographs, artwork, and a model of Cunard's beloved liner of the early 20th century. Three million dollars was spent achieving the art deco style. Tables and service stations were repositioned, opening up the restaurant, and making easier access for passengers and service staff. An International Food Bazaar allows passengers from each restaurant to sample food and drink from around the world.

Moving through the aft entrance of the Mauretania, you will find the 531-seat Theatre, surrounded on the starboard side by the comfortable Theatre Bar, with its adjacent dance floor, and on the port side by the Players Club Casino and Players Club Lounge. The casino is well equipped for those wishing to test their luck, with 2 roulette tables, 5 blackjack tables, and 68 slot machines. Nearby, two services that are used frequently by all *QE2* passengers are the Cruise Staff Office and the viewing area for photos taken by the ship's photographers, just aft of the casino.

The new Mauretania Restaurant (TOP) offers fine dining in an elegant and historic setting. The Players Club (BOTTOM LEFT) is one of the largest casinos afloat, while specialty shops (ABOVE) tempt the wallet in a different manner. This branch of Harrods is the only one to be found outside London.

The original design for the *Q3* project called for the Double Room to be separated into two lounges for second and third classes. As the design evolved, a two-deck main lounge was formed with a connecting circular staircase at the aft end of the room. For 17 years, the Double Room was the showplace for shipboard entertainment including the cabaret shows, dances, games, and lectures held on the *QE2*. The beautifully redesigned room has been fittingly named the Grand Lounge. A new twin staircase cascades down the forward end of the room, connecting Upper Deck with the shops on Boat Deck. Housed between is a new retractable stage with accompanying video, special effect lighting, and sound equipment. The seating is spread among three levels, greatly improving the passenger's view of the entertainment.

Further aft in the location of the former Double Down Bar, is the brand new Yacht Club. The centerpiece of the room is a stunning Schimmel baby grand piano encased by a clear Lucite top and matching counter. A new bar has been built using beautiful wood burr trim. The walls have been decorated with posters and models of vessels from the America's Cup races. Adjoining the Yacht Club are entertainment centers for the teens and adults. The Adult Center is a quiet area for cards, table shuffleboard, bumper pool, backgammon, and table tennis. The Teen Center is equipped with large-screen television, a video arcade, juke box and dance floor, and other game tables. During long cruises, the Teen Center is used as a Shore Excursion Office.

The new Grand Lounge (TOP), with its retractable stage and twin staircases, replaces the old Double Room. MIDDLE: Taking tea in the Queen's Grill Lounge. MIDDLE LEFT: Dinner in the intimate Princess Grill is the best way to begin the evening's activities. The Yacht Club, aft of the Grand Lounge (RIGHT), has become the new favored location to relax and watch the outdoor sports on Upper Deck.

Looking out from the Yacht Club, passengers can view the greatly enlarged Sporting Area. Paddle tennis, basketball, shuffleboard, quoits, a golf driving net, and putting green are all available.

At the forward end of Quarter Deck are the Princess Grill and Columbia Restaurant. The intimate 150-seat Princess Grill, located on the *QE2*'s port side, is accessed either by a private stairway or elevator in the Princess Grill Cocktail Bar on One Deck. The figures representing the four elements, originally done by Janine Janet for the Queen's Grill, are found in the Princess Grill. These statues were created using all organic materials such as shells, coral, and mother of pearl.

Leisure activities aboard the QE2 can include (TOP) a game of paddle tennis, (MIDDLE) practicing on the putting green, relaxing in a Jacuzzi (LEFT), or keeping fit at an aerobics class at the exclusive Golden Door Spa (BOTTOM LEFT).

The Club Lido (TOP) plays host to informative lectures and deck buffets at the Quarter Deck pool during the day, and night-time entertainment and disco dancing through the evening. The Card Room (BOTTOM) provides a quiet location for playing favorite board or card games. RIGHT: The soft leather cube chairs in the Queen's Room.

The Columbia Restaurant seats 750 passengers but is separated into smaller sections by six mirrored archways to provide a more private atmosphere. On display at the after entrance to the restaurant is the huge silver loving cup, which was presented to Samuel Cunard by the citizens of Boston upon the maiden voyage arrival of the *Britannia* in 1840. A new wooden dance floor has been added to the room for dinner dancing. On the port side, aft of the Columbia Restaurant, is the Library and Card Room. The library aboard the *Queen Elizabeth 2* is one of the best afloat, and the most beautiful. A professional librarian is on staff to help passengers select any of the 3,000 books, or check out games and activities. The Card Room incorporates many of the historical photographs, illustrations, and ship models formerly in the Reading Room on Boat Deck. The room provides the perfect setting for card playing, with its private booths and well-illuminated tables.

The Midships Bar is located on the starboard side, and has always been a favorite location for those passengers dining in the nearby Columbia Restaurant. Its elegant interior was designed by Dennis Lennon in dark green and black. The social center for first class passengers on the North Atlantic is the Queen's Room. High tea could not be served in a more elegant setting. Oscar Nemon's bust of Queen Elizabeth II overlooking the forward end of the room has been painted gold and surrounded by beautiful ash burl trim. The "trumpet chairs" which matched the inverted columns in the room have been replaced by soft leather cube chairs.

The multi-purpose Club Lido is located at the after end of Quarter Deck, with comfortable seating for lectures or relaxation. Two buffet serving areas allow passengers an alternative to the formal restaurants, and feature healthful foods recommended by The Golden Door. At night, passengers are invited by the flashing lights and glass dance floor of the Club Lido disco and adjoining cocktail bar. Through the sliding glass doors, the Magrodome allows pool-side viewing of the starry sky in warm comfort.

The passenger accommodations have not been left out of the massive refurbishment. Each one of the 951 staterooms and suites has been renewed or completely redesigned. A completely automated telephone exchange system has replaced the familiar operator. A multilingual verbal clock and automatic wake-up features are now available, and satellite ship-to-shore calls can be dialed direct.

All staterooms are now furnished with color television, with the Queen and Princess Grill staterooms further equipped with an audio-visual entertainment center comprising a 16-channel color television set and videotape player, remote control, and four audio channels. A video camera has been permanently mounted near the bridge for a constant view of what lies ahead of the ship. News and stock exchange information are continually accessible, as well as movies and entertainment in several languages. Grundig of Germany has installed an entire TV Control Room on Three Deck to coordinate and produce programming entertainment.

The Steiner's Beauty Salon and Barber Shop on One Deck has been enlarged and remodeled. This is often the passenger's first stop for looking his or her best.

The outdoor One Deck Pool has been enhanced by two new Jacuzzi whirlpools and a children's pool. If the outdoor life is not appealing, the Golden Door Spa at the Six Deck Pool offers three more Jacuzzis. The Seven Deck indoor pool is the location for the Golden Door's Nautilus and exercise equipment, massage and shower facilities.

Eight new suites (TOP) were added in 1987, bringing new decor to Signal Deck. The Magrodome over the Quarter Deck pool (BOTTOM) allows enjoyment in all types of weather.

PUT TO THE TEST

On April 8, just one day behind schedule, the *Queen Elizabeth 2* was ready for the first sea trials with her new engines in the North Sea. She carried 1,800 passengers, including 750 engineers from Lloyd Werft. The liner was slowly worked up to 21 knots, while vibration tests were made throughout the ship. Suddenly, the engines were shut down due to high temperatures in four propeller shaft bearings near the propulsion motors. It was discovered that they had been made several millimeters too small. A simple problem, but one which forced delay of any further testing until a helicopter could take the parts back to Bremerhaven for re-milling.

The shipyard completed the work quickly, and the *QE2* was soon underway again. The engines were again worked up to 21 knots, while experiments were made with various propeller pitch settings. The speed was then increased to an amazing 33.1 knots, faster than the *QE2,* or either of the prior *Queens*, had ever travelled before.

A new series of "crash tests" were carried out to test the effects of the new controllable pitch propellers. The *QE2* went from 30 knots to a complete stop in three minutes and forty-two seconds, using only 3/4 of a mile. Within another 12 minutes, the ship was travelling astern at an astounding 19 knots. On her previous tests in 1970, with the old propellers, the *QE2* took six and a half minutes to stop from 28.5 knots.

The *Queen Elizabeth 2*'s "second maiden voyage," like her first, was not without its share of troubles. Certain work on her interiors was not completed in time, necessitating workmen to sail with the ship to New York. A pipe burst, making several cabins uninhabitable. The large number of new crew members made service less proficient than the normally high Cunard standard. A few passengers complained to the media about the crossing, and Cunard Line decided to offer partial refunds for everyone's inconvenience. As with any maiden voyage, especially in the *QE2*'s case, time was needed to learn new equipment and procedures.

Now the *Queen Elizabeth 2* is better than ever, and continues to offer more than any other cruise ship in the world. She carries on the proud heritage of the previous *Queen* liners and legendary Cunard ships of the past, while leading today's cruise industry with the latest technology and amenities. With her latest re-fit, the Cunard Line has wisely enabled the *Queen Elizabeth 2* to continue giving her passengers the finest in ocean-going travel for decades to come.

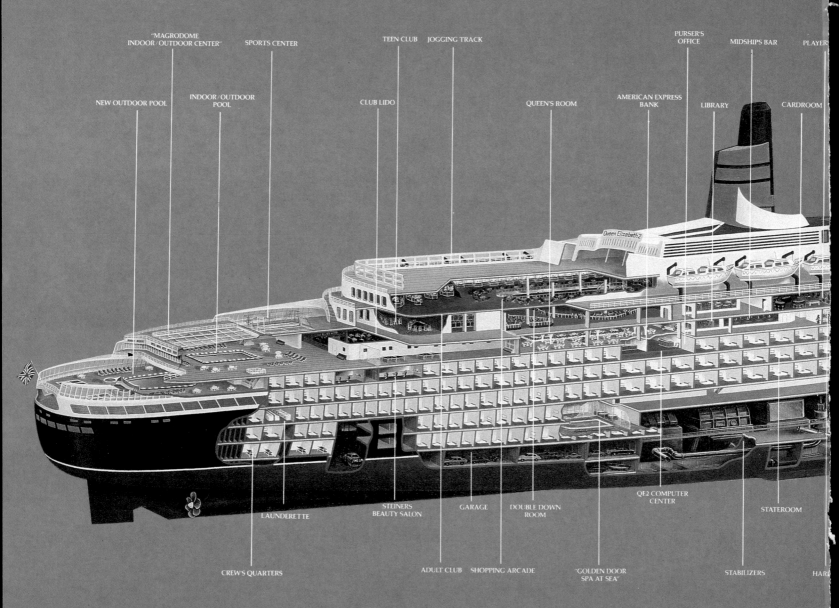

"MAGRODOME
INDOOR/OUTDOOR CENTER"
SPORTS CENTER
TEEN CLUB
JOGGING TRACK
PURSER'S
OFFICE
MIDSHIPS BAR
PLAYER'

NEW OUTDOOR POOL
INDOOR/OUTDOOR
POOL
CLUB LIDO
QUEEN'S ROOM
AMERICAN EXPRESS
BANK
LIBRARY
CARDROOM

Queen Elizabeth 2

LAUNDERETTE
STEINERS
BEAUTY SALON
GARAGE
DOUBLE DOWN
ROOM
QE2 COMPUTER
CENTER
STATEROOM

CREW'S QUARTERS
ADULT CLUB
SHOPPING ARCADE
"GOLDEN DOOR
SPA AT SEA"
STABILIZERS
HARE

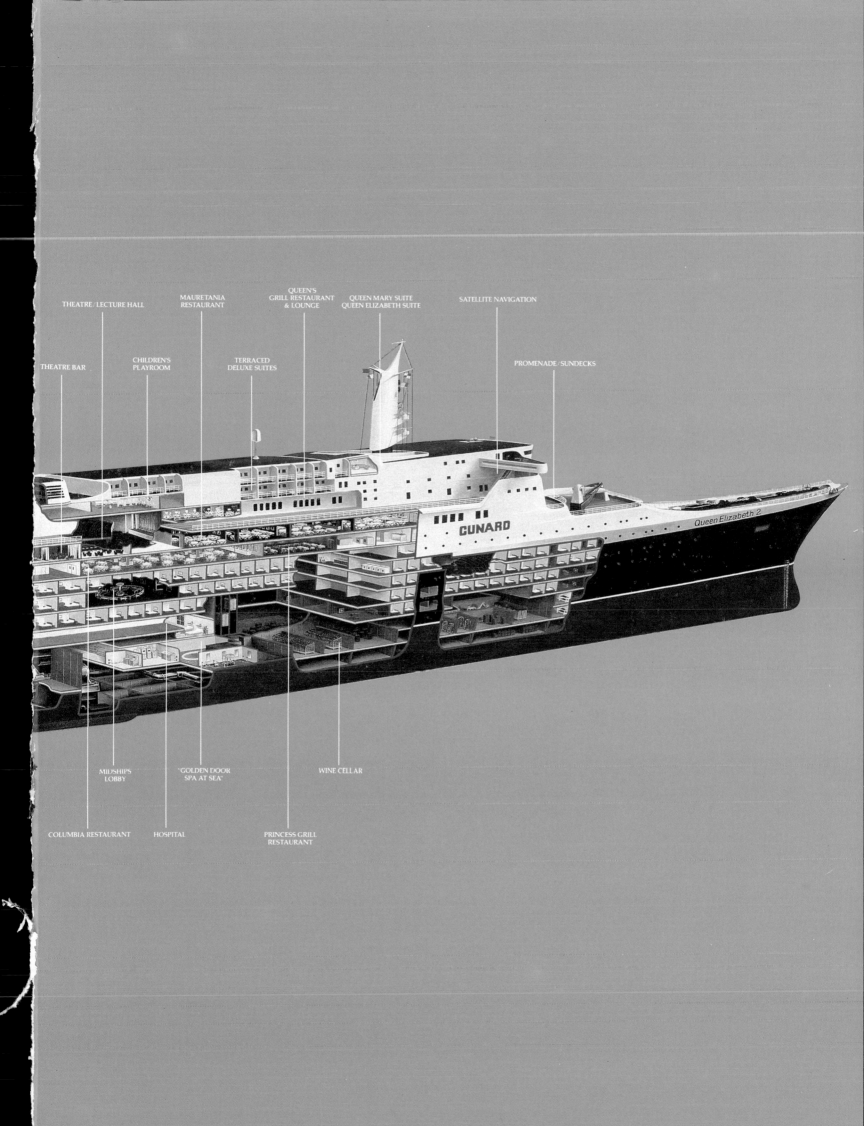

THEATRE/LECTURE HALL

MAURETANIA
RESTAURANT

QUEEN'S
GRILL RESTAURANT
& LOUNGE

QUEEN MARY SUITE
QUEEN ELIZABETH SUITE

SATELLITE NAVIGATION

THEATRE BAR

CHILDREN'S
PLAYROOM

TERRACED
DELUXE SUITES

PROMENADE/SUNDECKS

CUNARD

Queen Elizabeth 2

MIDSHIP'S
LOBBY

"GOLDEN DOOR
SPA AT SEA"

WINE CELLAR

COLUMBIA RESTAURANT

HOSPITAL

PRINCESS GRILL
RESTAURANT